"There has always been cosmic unity and ultimate meaning, not because human beings have made it up, but because it is simply so. We only have to access and become that already existent truth in awakened states of consciousness—in mystical and psychedelic ways, in particular. This is good news beyond the gospel, robust comparison outside the academic nay-saying, spirituality without the religions. It is exactly, fantastically what we need to hear, right now." —**Jeffrey J. Kripal**, J. Newton Rayzor Chair in Philosophy and Religious Thought, Rice University; author of *How to Think Impossibly*

"Dana Sawyer makes a persuasive case for the contemporary relevance of Perennialist Philosophy, not as dogmatic religious belief but as unitive mystical experience and provisional ideas about its nature and implications. Sawyer is to be applauded for his nuanced account, which dispels persistent misunderstandings and recognizes a variety of Perennialist perspectives on religion, God, spiritual awakening, nature, art, and much else. An indispensable, highly accessible introduction to Perennialist Philosophy and what it can be today." —**Paul Marshall, PhD**, author of *Mystical Encounters with the Natural World* and *The Shape of the Soul*

"The recent flurry of research articles on the therapeutic benefits of psychedelic medicines has focused on the therapeutic impact of the mystical experience. However the context has been medical, primarily about psychiatric symptom reduction. Professor Dana Sawyer, in *Perennial Philosophy Reloaded*, gives us a spiritual and ethical context for valuing a mystical experience. The book is a reader friendly tour of the Perennial Philosophy which is well-needed in our current cultural milieu. A must read for students of world religion, philosophy, psychedelic studies and those brave souls embarking on a spiritual path." —**Rachel Harris, PhD**, psychologist in private practice for thirty-five years, author of *Swimming in the Sacred*

"I am a neuroscientist who, through my own mystical experiences and research, have come to embrace Perennial Philosophy. Thus, I was intrigued to read The Perennial Philosophy Reloaded. Each chapter is a goldmine of information. I had difficulty putting it down. It captivated me with its wisdom and heart-opening ways of expressing that wisdom. It is truly a guide home for the mystically inclined." —**Marjorie Woollacott, PhD**, professor emerita, Institute of Neuroscience, University of Oregon; author of *Infinite Awareness: the Awakening of a Scientific Mind*

"Speaking to those who sense that a mysterious luminosity shines in and through everyone and everything, Sawyer articulates an eloquent defense of the intrinsic and transformative value of spiritual awakening and mystical experience." —**G. William Barnard**, professor of religious studies, Southern Methodist University; author of *Living Consciousness* and *Liquid Light*

"Dana Sawyer has done us the indispensable service of clearing the thicket of misunderstandings and simplifications surrounding the perennial philosophy, not only by mapping out the emergence of its recent variations, but by comparing these newer versions with one another and with earlier theories advocated by Aldous Huxley and the very different Traditionalist School of perennialism inspired by Rene Guenon and Frithjof Schuon. This is a book of astonishing spiritual breadth and depth and practical advice, applying the insights of older and newer perennialist traditions to raise questions and challenge our everyday assumptions about who we are and what is the goal of our life. Sawyer helpfully weaves together insights and wisdom from philosophy, psychology, world religions, the hard sciences, and the history of mysticism on the mystery of consciousness, thereby providing us with a rich font of information on seminal figures and thought-provoking ideas that we may draw on to help us on our own spiritual quest." —**Bradley Malkovsky**, associate professor, University of Notre Dame; former editor, Journal of *Hindu-Christian Studies*

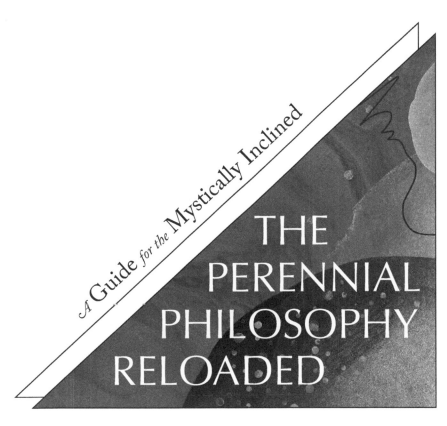

THE
PERENNIAL
PHILOSOPHY
RELOADED

A Guide for the Mystically Inclined

Dana Sawyer

Monkfish Book Publishing Company
Rhinebeck, New York

Paperback ISBN 978-1-958972-29-8
eBook ISBN 978-1-958972-30-4

Library of Congress Cataloging-in-Publication Data

Names: Sawyer, Dana, 1951- author.
Title: The perennial philosophy reloaded : a guide for the mystically
    inclined / Dana Sawyer.
Description: Rhinebeck, New York : Monkfish Book Publishing Company, [2024]
Identifiers: LCCN 2023050295 (print) | LCCN 2023050296 (ebook) | ISBN
    9781958972298 (paperback) | ISBN 9781958972304 (ebook)
Subjects: LCSH: Religion--Philosophy. | Philosophy and religion.
Classification: LCC BL51 .S4135 2024 (print) | LCC BL51 (ebook) | DDC
    210--dc23/eng/20240422
LC record available at https://lccn.loc.gov/2023050295
LC ebook record available at https://lccn.loc.gov/2023050296

Cover painting "Exit Through the Looking Glass" by Dana Sawyer
Book and cover design by Colin Rolfe

Monkfish Book Publishing Company
22 East Market Street, Suite 304
Rhinebeck, New York 12572
(845) 876-4861
monkfishpublishing.com

To my grandson Rhys

"The real voyage of discovery consists not in seeking new land-scapes but in having new eyes."

Marcel Proust

"What is that which gleams through me and smites my heart without wounding it? I am both a-shudder and a-glow."

St. Augustine

"My soul is from elsewhere, I'm sure of that, and I intend to end up there."

Jalal ud-Din Rumi

CONTENTS

INTRODUCTION

Where do we come from? What are we? Where are we going? This is the title of a painting by the French post-impressionist Paul Gauguin, and although it was painted in Tahiti in 1897, it refers to a set of questions that have arisen in the human mind and heart everywhere and always since we first looked up at the stars and wondered. Most of us, at one time or another, find ourselves asking, What is happening to me?, Why is this happening?, and What is the nature of this place where all this is happening to me? Furthermore, given that we are purposeful creatures, we also wonder, *Is there any real meaning or purpose to this?* Collectively, we might call these queries the short list of life's biggest questions. They're big principally because they have a quality of ultimate importance.

Life is filled with mundane circumstances that make us wonder and question but that—unlike the big questions—have no *ultimate* importance. For instance, we might ask: why do most songs on the radio have a three-minute format? Or even more mundane: what's for dinner? We have goals and purposes that are of a less-than-ultimate nature, like taking out the trash or feeding our pets. But the majority of us, at least every now and then, also feel the need to place these and other matters inside a larger context, that is, inside an ultimate concern that gives all our thoughts and actions a point of reference and a touchstone for richer meaning and purpose in life. For example, Buddhists formulate the direction of their lives around the ultimate goal of reaching *nirvana* (spiritual awakening), while Christians act in ways they hope will lead them to heaven and salvation. Secular Humanists, for their part, seek to create a just and equitable society here on earth.

Given all this, what if we personally don't think we have an ultimate concern or primary goal to inform our everyday actions and interests? What if we don't believe in a specific religion or fixed ideology? My take is that an identifiable ultimate concern or ultimate goal—however roughly drawn or provisionally held—lies within each of us, even if it's no more complex than the desire to enjoy ourselves physically, i.e., the concern of Epicureans. I have joked with my students that if an anthropologist was invisible and followed them around every day for a month, writing down everything they did, it would be possible to extrapolate from their actions their general values and worldview. Is the person environmentally concerned? Is time spent in nature a priority for them? What do their morals look like? Where do they stand on social issues? And so on and so forth. Your behavior too would reveal answers to these questions. In short, we can hold an ultimate concern even if we're not consciously aware of it—which is the case for many people in the world. We may hold onto the views we inherited from our family and culture—often accepted and expressed robotically—or we may find new ones of our own. Either way, a compass for finding meaning and purpose is discernible in our everyday actions. Everything we do is expressive of our inherent ideology, whether we hold it consciously or unconsciously.

Paul Tillich, the Christian theologian who coined the term "Ultimate Concern" as a way of summarizing a person's answers to life's biggest questions, argued that a sense of deeper purpose and richer context is so important to us as humans that without an Ultimate Concern we are in danger of losing our will to live, of losing what he called our "courage to be," leading toward a life of slovenly, random, and often self-destructive behavior. Without an ultimate meaning and purpose to guide and inspire our actions, we simply run out of gas, stalling out along life's highway.

In strong resonance with Tillich's viewpoint, Viktor Frankl, an Austrian psychiatrist who survived the Nazi death camps at Auschwitz and Dachau, once described (in *Man's Search for Meaning*, 1946) how those Jews who lost their faith as a result of the horrors they were forced to endure could no longer endure them, perishing from lack of a sense of meaning beyond the horror. Conversely, Frankl himself did not lose faith, and, as a consequence, survived. Later he argued that the perennial arising of the same set of life's biggest questions, and the same driving need to find answers to them—which exists in all cultures everywhere—suggests that life *does* have an implicit meaning. The questions themselves imply they have answers, for otherwise what would be the evolutionary value of our perpetually asking them?

Whether or not we agree with Frankl's last point, he and Tillich were entirely useful in pointing out how prevalent the search for meaning is, and how endemic it is to our everyday behavior—again, whether we're aware of it or not.

Continuing our first look at life's biggest questions, we may feel frustrated that our life didn't begin with a clearly laid out plan or Ultimate Concern. Why weren't we given a download of answers to all of life's questions at birth? Why all this groping in the dark where, as Huston Smith, the renowned scholar of world religions, once remarked, we are confronted with life like a Rorschach ink blot test, revealing no specific interpretation? Is there an evolutionary purpose to having us figure everything out for ourselves? Is the mystery of life even decipherable? What if Frankl and Tillich are completely wrong and there's no purpose to our existence at all—as Sartre and Camus, the French existentialists, were once convinced?

This book contends that Frankl and Tillich were right to say that life has inherent meaning—though the *form* of that meaning, as we'll see, is experiential rather than didactic or concept based, allowing for much leeway in terms of interpretation. I will offer answers to life's biggest questions from the perspective of what's called "The Perennial Philosophy," and these answers will derive mainly from the shared viewpoints of Aldous Huxley, Alan Watts, Huston Smith, Frances Vaughan, Stanislav Grof, and Ram Dass, all of whose theories sit under this broad philosophical umbrella. Other authors will be mentioned (including contemporary Perennialists), but the views of these six theorists form our primary reference points. I won't always refer to their work specifically, but their shared outlook is endemic to all that is to follow.

Collectively, their Perennialist views center on the value of a particular type of mystical experience—specifically, an awakening into a sense of our unity with all reality. These authors believed we have a latent, though often undeveloped, capacity to experience deeper levels of our being, revealing insights and understandings lying outside our generally blinkered view of what we are and our place in the world. They believed the truth of life is not a collection of facts, nor a religious dogma, nor a memorized system of philosophy (even including *their* philosophy), but rather an experiential truth based in a state of expanded consciousness akin to the sense of cosmic oneness described by mystics of myriad religions. The truth of life, as these authors—and the mystics themselves—conceived it, is seeing with new eyes rather than simply entertaining new ideas.

I mention the mystical writings of the world's religions, but Perennialists, including those cited above, aren't necessarily interested in organized religion (more on this in the "Religion" chapter). In general, they believe the religions are very different one from the other, with few if any commonalities; however, they also contend there is a particular type of extraordinary experience running like a thread through many of their mystical traditions. Each describes a variety of non-ordinary experiences and paranormal states of consciousness, and each may place different weights and values on these experiences. However, a wide range of mystics have described a particularly valuable experience of "union with ultimate reality" or "oneness with the divine principle" or "merger with God" that Perennialists see as—using Aldous Huxley's term—the "highest common factor" of the mystical traditions. It is an experience that many mystics not only shared but that they believed affords the broadest insight, giving the most benefit for daily life. This book is all about why this is so.

Giving just a brief preview of what's ahead, the Perennialist mystics argued that mystical experience is a direct experience of ourselves as fundamentally entwined with the universe. During the unitive experience, they say, we know the deepest level of our being as inseparable from the deepest level of *all* being.

Rather than trying to access truth via the rational mind, as philosophers (including me) generally attempt to do, Perennialists have grasped life's truth through direct experience, something William James, a founder of modern psychology, termed an experience of "noetic" insight, derived from the Greek word *noesis* meaning "inner knowing." Here, now, I'm speaking about the experiences of such mystics as Jalal ud-Din Rumi, Teresa of Avila, Adi Shankara, Lao Tzu, Moses de Leon, Mirabai, Meister Eckhart, and the Buddha, for though they came from different religious traditions and cultures, if we compare their key experiences, and to a large extent even their interpretations of those experiences, we find something approaching parity—and familiarity with what would come from those who formed the perennial philosophy in the twentieth century. These mystics did not see this experience, the *unitive mystical experience* (UME), as the only type of mystical experience, but many (and arguably most) *did* see it as the one having the greatest benefit, and their experiences helped form their answers to life's biggest questions.

Perennialists also argue that the noetic insight gained during UMEs has arisen everywhere and always because it is timelessly woven into the fabric of our very natures and the fabric of nature itself. Hence, the *perennial* aspect of the perennial philosophy, in that it is eternally present in our existential relationship to the world. While the religions may — and do — differ, their mystics often closely agree on key descriptions related to this shared experience of oneness with reality, nature, or God (I realize that these words are all loaded with varying meanings), and this book focuses on those points of agreement, offering a condensed guide to what life's about from the perspective of the perennial philosophy. Therefore, the thread we will follow deals mainly with three questions: (1) What is the nature of the experience of unity or oneness with reality? (2) How does that experience provide answers to life's biggest questions? (3) And, what are the actual benefits of knowing these answers?

One point to make clear at the beginning is that I'll be speaking in general terms. I already have been doing so. One can do no other in a book such as this, without losing readers in the weeds.

Contrary to the view of its detractors, the perennial philosophy is not a monolithic position affording only one view, but rather a family of theories. There are commonalities and a distinct family resemblance between the various systems, but there is also disagreement and variety. In brief, the perennial philosophy is a category much like existentialism, phenomenology, idealism, or post-modernism, referring to a collection of related viewpoints, and as such it's important not to confuse one iteration of it for the position in general. My goal is to give the viewpoint held in common by the majority of Perennialists, but I will also point out differences of opinion on various details, such as views on organized religion, to make clear why perennial philosophers cannot—and *should* not—be considered as homogeneous, and the perennial philosophy not a siloed school of thought. In fact, one reason why I've "reloaded" the Perennialist family of theories is to make that clear.

During my several decades of teaching philosophy and world religions at the college level, students have often asked me to share what I think is true, philosophically speaking, about life. They've offered comments such as, "Well, you've been studying philosophy and religion for years and years, so by now you must have some sort of best guess about things. What do you think life is about?"

From time to time I've shared my thoughts, out of sympathy for our shared desire to find meaning in life. There are times in this age of DIY (Do-It-Yourself) spirituality when we all feel the need to compare notes along the way. It's in that spirit that I share my views in this book (as I shared them with students), with the hope of explaining what made sense to me as a possible resource for you—and, as I always told my students, if my ideas don't seem useful, don't keep them. You're on your own journey through life, so you must decide for yourself what works.

Another reason I wrote this book has to do with the fact that the perennial philosophy is increasingly popular in our culture, forming a cultural trend worth noting. At academic conferences, colleagues have in the past enjoyed telling me that perennial philosophy, popular back in the 1960s, is no longer relevant. They've encouraged me to "Get out of the hippie thing" or "Forget about Aldous Huxley and Alan Watts" or "Grow up and smell the meaninglessness!" In short, they've wanted me to face the fact that the perennial philosophy has either been disproven or forgotten. However, I couldn't and still can't face their music, because it doesn't ring true.

First off, I don't agree with my colleagues because the perennial philosophy is an entirely defensible position, philosophically speaking. The reasons why I say this actually go beyond the scope of this book, but let me add for now that—as I have argued in academic journals—having closely critiqued the arguments against perennial philosophy for more than twenty years, most of its detractors have either glossed the position or misunderstood it altogether. Furthermore, I don't feel compelled to put aside the perennial philosophy on the grounds that it's no longer relevant because I find it alive and well in the current spiritual zeitgeist. A few scholars may have set it aside, but I find it very prevalent in the so-called "consciousness movement."

For instance, we find general principles of Perennialism in the works of living authors (at my time of writing) such as Deepak Chopra, Ken Wilber, Richard Rohr, Marianne Williamson, Stanislav Grof, Tara Brach, Andrew Harvey, William Richards, Rupert Spira, Gabor Mate, Mirabai Starr, Rabbi Rami Shapiro, Dean Radin, Joan Borysenko, and a host of others. Don't worry if you don't recognize these authors, but I imagine you do know at least a few of them. They collectively attract a huge audience and their views generally resonate with Perennialism.

I also suggest that even though the perennial philosophy hasn't been part of the dominant ideology of western culture, historically speaking, it has, for more than 200 years been a *recessive viewpoint* arising over and over again in our culture: discernible, for instance, in the views of thinkers and opinion-influencers of a century or more ago including Friedrich Schiller, Friedrich Schelling, Samuel Taylor Coleridge, Ralph Waldo Emerson, Henry David Thoreau, Walt Whitman, and William James. And yes, this viewpoint was again strongly evident in our culture starting in the 1960s. (Don't knock the Sixties!)

To my mind, one reason why this recessive fascination with inner knowing and expanded consciousness keeps resurfacing is the same reason that mystics of all cultures have come upon it: it rises naturally and rings true when the unitive mystical experience occurs. And because it rings true and keeps arising, it is worth understanding, so that we, as individuals and a culture, can not only recognize it but explore its possibilities. Why discard out of hand what keeps arising and promises such value?

Perennial philosophy has strong appeal for many people today for the same reasons it first appealed to me. Specifically, perennial philosophy is reloading in our time because it:

- ► Asks for no faith claim;
- ► Contains no views that contradict scientific facts or confound rational principles;

- ▶ Requires no adherence to a dogma; and
- ▶ Neither includes nor requires membership in any sort of formal organization or church.

This last characteristic has strong appeal for those who identify today as "spiritual but not religious," and who visit retreat centers where expertise is respected but hierarchical authority is avoided. This brings me to my last reason for writing this book.

Today we are in the midst of what Ben Sessa and many others have called the "psychedelic renaissance," a rebirth of interest in psychedelic experience, not only for its possible therapeutic value but for its growth potential relative to the lives of "healthy normals"—which, after all, is most of us. For thirty years, between 1970 and 2000, our society's fears about psychedelics were so intense that even scientific research with these substances was made illegal. But for nearly a quarter century since that time, studies at Johns Hopkins, New York University, Columbia, Yale, Harvard and elsewhere have revealed strong evidence of their value. Consequently, the general public is increasingly interested in how psychedelic experience might benefit their lives. Those who have experimented with the substances have generally found them useful for personal growth, and given that fact, today we are undergoing a grand search for interpretations of psychedelic experience—including the unitive mystical experience, which commonly occurs during psychedelic journeys.

All of the authors I've cited as my primary touchstones (Huxley, Watts, Smith, Vaughan, Grof, and Ram Dass) were renowned psychedelic explorers of the first wave, back in the 1950s and 1960s, and each of them interpreted their unitive experiences in terms related to Huxley's iteration of the perennial philosophy. Other interpretations of the UME are possible (given that psychedelic experience is a variety of life experience, and life, as we know, is hard to pin down), but I will argue that perennialism, speaking in broad terms, and with no settled opinion on the details, offers a compelling interpretation of the UME, whether that experience is triggered by psychedelics or in some other way. Cutting to the chase, if you're interested or involved in today's psychedelic rebirth, you're likely to find the perennial philosophy deeply interesting.

Just before we begin, let me say something about the structure of this book. Part I is comprised of the first three chapters, which together give a brief overview of the perennial philosophy and its relevance for today. This section can be read as a stand-alone introduction to the subject but it is intended to be like the overture of a symphony, providing a taste of what's to follow in Part II. Part II, made up of chapters 4 through 7, is the heart of the book, expanding on Part I by discussing the perennial philosophy as it directly relates to life's biggest questions, specifically: (1) What is happening to us?; (2) Where are we? (put another way, What is the nature of this world in which we find ourselves?); (3) Where are we going? (or What's our ultimate goal or purpose?); and finally, (4) How can we get there?

After exploring answers to these questions, Part III continues the inquiry by discussing Perennialism's implications for such topics as the future of religion, the importance of love and interpersonal relationships, the nature of spiritual awakening, theories of our psychological make-up, the significance of art, and the value (if any) of psychedelic drugs for the process of spiritual growth. These last chapters, by the way, can be read out of sequence, allowing you to decide which topics most interest you. But if you decide to read one or more chapters of Part III, I recommend reading all of Parts I and II first, since they provide the foundation for what's to follow. In addition, I strongly recommend reading the last chapter on "The Perennial Philosophy Today" as well as the short Epilogue.

And so let's begin!

PART
ONE

Starting Out

1

WHAT'S *REALLY* GOING ON?

"My brain is only a receiver; in the Universe there is a core from which we obtain knowledge, strength and inspiration. I have not penetrated into the secrets of this core, but I know that it exists."

Nikola Tesla

Many years ago, while studying Asian religions at the University of Iowa, I was camping with a group of friends and we were seated around a campfire. Out of the darkness from behind us, a friend returned to the group from setting up his tent and yelled to nobody in particular, "I want to know what's *really* going on!" Everyone laughed but me. For me, his comment triggered one of those eureka moments when you feel like you've somehow been pinched awake. I felt struck by a thunderbolt of insight. All my motivations for studying religion and philosophy—and even for camping and hiking—flooded into my mind. It was because I didn't only want to know what was going on in my life, I wanted to know what was *really* going on. After my friend made his exclamation, I yelled back at him, "Me too!", which triggered another burst of laughter from our friends.

Of course, what some people believe is really going on is that nothing is going on at all. In 1999, while visiting a colleague in Japan, my wife and I found ourselves sharing a beer one evening with some Brits at a bar in Osaka. The Brits were there to sell drill presses to a large Japanese company and one of the guys asked me what I did for a living. "I teach philosophy and world religions," I replied.

"Well," he remarked with a giggle, "that's a waste of time, isn't it."

I took no offense; I could see he meant the comment in fun, although he *was* serious about his point. I asked for his reason in believing I was wasting my time and he answered, "Because that stuff is all about finding truth and meaning, right?" When I agreed it was, he continued, "Well, there's nothing to find, is there? It's like looking for rocking horse poop; there's nothing to find." We all chuckled at the analogy and the conversation quickly moved to other subjects, but I took note that the guy was expressing a commonly held opinion. Many people today believe the truth of life is that there is no truth of life. Our lives (and life in general) are simply the result of natural selection and chance mutation, having no inherent meaning or purpose whatsoever.

Of course, one of the challenges of holding this position is that, in some sense at least, meaning is not only useful for finding purpose in life, *it's also entirely unavoidable.* The French philosopher Maurice Merleau-Ponty once expressed his reason for this same claim with the following observation: "Because we are present to a world, we are condemned to meaning." His point was that soon after we're born, we come to realize we are in a relationship with a world of people and things extending beyond ourselves, and our forced need to interact with this world—a world of *others*—demands that we consider how we should interact with it. Furthermore, and in agreement with Merleau-Ponty's position, no matter what we decide, we inescapably base all of our values and actions on what we've decided—or unconsciously inherited as the decisions of our culture. In brief, we base our actions on what we believe has most value for us and is therefore most meaningful to us. And even those of us who say life is meaningless are not let off the hook, for they too must interact with this world of others, and consequently, if they base their actions on their assumption that life is meaningless, this is simply a case of finding meaninglessness meaningful. It is their faith in nothingness and meaninglessness that directs their behavior—including, in the case of Sartre and Camus, a desire to convince others that life is meaninglessness. In short, there's no escape from choosing meaning; we must act and our meanings are revealed in our actions. We are choosing a platform of meaning all the time, whether we like it or not. Beginning in the 1980s, much of popular music expressed the view that life lacks meaning (you may remember "Mad World" by the

British band Tears for Fears) and many of my Gen X students embraced this viewpoint, even as I had once been an existentialist of the Camus and Sartre sort. Over the past thirty years, I've taken an informal poll that suggests more than three-quarters of my students have believed life's only meaning is whatever purpose they personally assign to it, with no inherent purpose beyond the biological drives of eating, sleeping, going to the toilet, and having sex. And, frankly, I can sympathize with why they have thought so.

First, because the search for meaning can be frustrating, producing so much confusion and insecurity that we feel pressured either to drop the search altogether (but remember Merleau-Ponty argued that we can't) or find something we can easily grasp onto. This pressure can result in clutching too quickly, and with little serious reflection, onto whichever religion or philosophy is readily at hand, often from the dominant ideology of our family and society. And this is why Arabs tend to be Muslims, Italians tend to be Catholics, and the Chinese tend to be Communists. It is also the reason why teens in the U.S., especially in the past thirty years, have tended to be cynical on the subject of life's purpose. So much of the music aimed at them has conveyed such messages as, "Life is a death sentence from which there's no escape!"; "The Man is out to get you!"; "Spirituality is a bunch of woo woo bullshit!"; "Humans suck and you suck too!"; and, "You should probably kill yourself, though killing yourself will be as meaningless as all your other actions!" Perhaps they listened to the same radio stations as the British guy in Osaka I mentioned earlier. We are all attracted to the chance for philosophical certainty (even if, paradoxically, what we become certain of is uncertainty itself) and philosophical directives are readily available to us—in fact, popular culture bombards us with them daily.

Exploring the topic of the prevalent cynicism a bit more deeply (given that it's the default philosophical position of many people today), let me add just a few more details. First, we can take note of how attractive cynicism and nihilism can be, psychologically speaking. They deliver a sense of certainty without calling on us to defend any well-articulated viewpoint; we can simply doubt the truth claims of everyone else, justifying our behavior on the basis of the notion that "all actions are ultimately pointless, so why not do as I please?" But the enticements and rewards of thinking cynically (and, of course, there is a definite downside) are not only psychological; they are cultural, which, after all, is why they're on the radio.

Specifically, when considering what's the best informed and most scientifically viable assessment of what's really going on, many people have arrived at the conclusion that our lives are devoid of inherent meaning. Life, generally speaking, is the search for something to keep you occupied until you die, whether or not it's also sometimes pleasant or fun. Life, in short, is busy work. But what if this position, prevalent as it has become, is simply wrong? What if life has an inherent meaning and value but it's delivered mainly through a level of consciousness or noetic experience that our society has not trained us to access?

Perennialists believe that is the case. Our present situation, they contend, is analogous to that of the prisoners in Plato's Cave. In *The Republic*, Plato relates an allegory of slaves who are chained in a dimly lit cave, forced to watch shadows play across the wall in front of them. Since they are chained and unable to turn around, they can't see who is making the shadows, nor do they recognize the shadows as shadows. They think the shadow world in front of them is the whole story of reality. Plato argued that we are like those prisoners, bound by our assumptions into mistaking what we currently see and comprehend for all that it's possible to see and comprehend. Extending his allegory to our own situation, we assume that our minds and our five senses are showing us all of what's really going on, though, in Plato's opinion, we are complacently satisfying ourselves with a partial and misleading view.

Perennialists, as well as the majority of mystics from the past, believe there's another world to live in outside Plato's Cave, an illuminated landscape that is pregnant with purpose, meaning, and value. That is what's *really* going on while we content ourselves with a partial view. And though apprehending this bigger world (actually an expanded vision of our world) may transcend our current state of mind, the noetic awakening that brings it into focus does not contradict the laws of science (which is an important point for most Perennialists, as we'll discuss in Part III). But how do we access this world of light beyond Plato's Cave? That is the subject of our next chapter.

2

WAKING UP

"[T]he thesis that there is a distinctive kind of mystical experience that is cross-culturally pervasive is well supported."

Philip Goff, contemporary philosopher
of consciousness studies

"What higher grades of significance, what profound meanings and messages, does the world give us that we are overlooking? It is said that to a sage the leaves on the trees are like the pages of a sacred text, filled with transcendent meaning. We do not see things only as they are, but also as we are."

Roger Walsh, professor of psychiatry

$\mathcal{P}$*hilosophy, as an* academic discipline, has many areas of inquiry, for instance logic, ethics, ontology (dealing with the nature of existence), and aesthetics. Another of these sub-disciplines is epistemology, the "study of knowledge," including the methods by which we know what we know. If I tell you it's going to rain this afternoon, you might ask me how I know. Since there are various ways of knowing things, I might say, "I heard it on the radio" or "My barometer indicates the atmospheric pressure is dropping" or "My neighbor's cows are lying down in her field." The point I want to make here is that there are different ways of knowing and Perennialists argue that we've overlooked one of the most significant—that is, the way of noetic insight or inner knowing.

The Perennialists' preferred addition to our ways of gaining knowledge is not reason-based, and so it is not rational. But it is also not *irrational*. It is a method that doesn't rely on logic or concepts to achieve its insights and yet it still makes sense, in that its value for our lives can be rationally explained and defended. In brief, it's better to call this additional method *non-rational* rather than irrational. It is a way of discerning reality from the inside out, rather than the other way around (as does science) and has traditionally been termed "mystical" knowing. It has also been called, as I've said, "noetic" or inner knowing, dealing with an apprehension of what exists beyond the limits of the senses, in that realm of reality traditional cultures have termed the Sacred or metaphysical.

This particular way of knowing relies on an expansion of consciousness or, as the French novelist Marcel Proust put it, on "having new eyes." In the west today, we are very interested in what consciousness (our field of awareness) can reveal when focused on the external world. For instance, if we focus our awareness on plants we can build a system of botany, and if we focus it on rocks we can build a system of geology. But mystics of all traditions have been interested in what we might call the nature of consciousness itself. What is this light inside our heads that the philosopher Colin McGinn has called the "mysterious flame?" In the same way that we acknowledge an external world to be explored, mystics have recognized an internal wilderness, also to be explored—and with rich reward.

In the western world, we've mainly assumed that consciousness, whatever might be its nature, is a fixed commodity. Fundamentally, we are either awake or we are not awake, and we're all generally awake to the same degree. That's the general assumption. But in the mystical traditions, there is the view that consciousness is a variable; consequently and furthermore, some people are more awake—or more richly awake—than others.

To use an analogy, in the west we've traditionally or habitually assumed that consciousness operates like a standard light switch on the wall; it can be turned either on or off, and so we are awake during the day and "off" during the night. However, in the mystical traditions, it's believed that consciousness can vary greatly, functioning more like a dimmer switch; that is, the "light" of our consciousness can be turned "on" but it can also be turned "up," increasing its luminosity. Consequently, adherents of these traditions believe there are methods for expanding consciousness and by using these tools we can turn up our inner dimmer switch from a "not very bright" condition to one of awakening or "enlightenment." In enlightenment, the mystics tell us, we wake up from our everyday consciousness into a richer and more authentic apprehension of our existence, and of *all* existence—like prisoners who have escaped from Plato's Cave into the full sunshine of what lies beyond.

Referencing a particular religious tradition for a moment, "Buddha" is actually an honorific title derived from the Sanskrit verb root *budh*, "to awaken," and means "awakened." The Buddha was given this title as the "Awakened One" (his actual name was Siddhartha Gotama), because he was said to have woken up *all the way*, and this state of illumined mind—with his "dimmer switch" turned all the way up—revealed to him what was "*really going on*" in life. Consequently, Buddhists believe the deepest project of our lives is to wake up to a state of consciousness that reveals more fully what we actually *are* and what actually *is,* and mystics of myriad traditions have shared this goal. For instance, this same shift in consciousness is, according to Christian mystics like St. John of the Cross, Thomas Traherne, William Law, John Ruysbroeck, and Thomas Merton, the prerequisite to the perception of "a new heaven and a new earth," and may also reveal the "transcendent meaning" hidden in the leaves of the trees mentioned by Roger Walsh at the beginning of this chapter.

This upgrade into an awakened state of consciousness is called *sahaja samadhi* in Hinduism, *nirvana* in Buddhism, *sekhel mufla* in Kabbala (Jewish mysticism), the *beatific vision* in Christianity, and *baqa wa fana* in Sufi Islam. Over the past century, several philosophers, including William James, Rudolf Otto, D.T. Suzuki and W.T. Stace, have attempted to describe this state's general characteristics, compiling various but related typologies based on written testimonies. Later, in 1962, Walter Pahnke, working at Harvard, collated these typologies into a list of common characteristics, outlining the phenomenology of what the mystics generally experienced during their moments of breakthrough. His list included: (1) *Unity,* or a deeply felt sense of connectedness to all of life; (2) *Transcendence* of space and time; (3) a deeply felt *Positive mood* (the feeling, as Aldous Huxley once put it, that "Everything is ultimately All Right, capital A, Capital R"); (4) a sense of *Sacredness* and Holiness; (5) *Objectivity* and Reality, or the sense that what is happening is real in the deepest sense; (6) *Paradoxicality,* meaning, for instance, that one might simultaneously feel during the experience infinitely significant and insignificant; (7) *Ineffability*, or the inability to describe fully what one is experiencing in the light outside Plato's Cave because what is apprehended exists beyond our usual conceptual categories of experience; (8) *Transiency*, referring to the tendency of the beatific vision to be of brief duration (more on this later); and finally, (9) *Persisting positive changes* in one's attitude and behavior.

Related to this last characteristic, the experience shared by the mystics was not some sort of flash in the pan with no lasting effects; it triggered a comprehensive breakthrough in their sense of what is real, affecting not only how they viewed the world but how they lived their lives. Following their upgrade in consciousness, none of these mystics went back to business as usual; their mystical experience improved their outlook and behavior.

Perennialists are of the opinion that behavior improves because human life—in its very nature—has an inherent goal, and mystical awakening, especially in its form as the unitive mystical experience (UME), reveals that goal. Enlightenment sets life into a fresh context triggered by a broader perspective on what life's about. In the mystical literature we are told that most people, most of the time, are experiencing a limited view of their circumstances, and therefore living a life of *maya* or "illusion," to use a term borrowed from Buddhism and Hinduism. Buddhists aren't saying that what we are experiencing right now isn't really happening; they are saying that we are misinterpreting what's happening due to our limited awareness of what's really going on. However, after an upgrade in consciousness, this partial view is placed inside a broader context (as would leaving Plato's Cave cause the prisoners to reinterpret their experience of the Cave in new ways), catalyzing a revolution in our assessment of reality. With reference to the fifth characteristic of mystical experience, *Objectivity*, this new assessment has a sense of ultimacy about it, causing us to downgrade what we had previously believed was the whole story of our lives. Enlightenment, the mystics tell us, is a revolution in consciousness as dramatic as waking up from a dream.

But what is it, exactly, that enlightenment reveals? If "waking up" is a useful epistemology or method for uncovering what's really going on, what is it that we know in that elevated state of consciousness? What did the Buddha wake up *to*? This brings us to the central content of the perennial philosophy.

3

THE MINIMUM WORKING HYPOTHESIS

"[E]very emptiness we feel is Being eclipsed; all restlessness
a flailing for the Being that we need; all joy the evidence of
Being found."

Huston Smith

Aldous Huxley once outlined his particular version of the perennial philosophy in what he termed "the minimum working hypothesis." Having read widely in the world's mystical literature, he saw a thread of experience running across the various traditions. Specifically, he saw that many of the mystics had placed a premium on what Huxley termed the "unitive knowledge," which was the sense that they had merged into a oneness with God/ Nature/ the Sacred or Ultimate Reality. Huxley also noted that despite the fact that the unitive mystical experience (UME) was then weighed and evaluated variously inside the different religious traditions, the mystics themselves valued it. Furthermore, though they described and interpreted their experiences with a measure of differences related to their cultural backgrounds, there were also definitely similarities. Noting these similarities, Huxley drafted a theory of what the mystics' experiences and interpretations held in common, beginning with their agreement that the unitive experience matters more than any theory about it. Huxley then listed four postulates, paraphrased here, as a workable description of what the mystic's interpretations of their UMEs held in common:

THAT there is a transcendent foundation of all reality or
what Huxley termed the "Divine Ground of Being," existing beyond the physical world of time and space.

THAT this Ground of Being is transcendent to the world of time and space but also is manifest *as* the world of time and space. Consequently, it is both transcendent and immanent with no ultimate or impermeable separation between these two aspects of itself.

THAT it is possible for human beings not only to understand theories about this configuration of reality, but, via the "unitive knowledge," with its heightened state of consciousness, to experience it.

THAT achieving this spiritual awakening of our oneness with Ultimate Reality not only brings meaning and purpose to our lives, via a richer perspective on our circumstances in the world, but an awakening of our responsibilities toward others.

The "unitive knowledge," as a noetic apprehension of reality, and the four postulates for interpreting that experience, form the thread of what Huxley believed he saw across and between the world's mystical traditions. Subsequently, this formed the foundation that many Perennialists later built upon, including Watts, Vaughan, Grof, Ram Dass, and Huston Smith. So let's take a brief look at each of Huxley's postulates to better understand their proposed value for our lives.

To begin, the Perennialist position, in general—and not just Huxley's iteration of it—is correctly labeled in philosophy a form of "absolute idealism," in that it describes a comprehensive view of the way things *really* are that includes a metaphysical component, specifically a component that is the platform from which all the universe arises. Though this metaphysical foundation cannot be apprehended by the senses or directly measured by science (since it has no physical forms or *quanta* to be apprehended or measured by science), it is always present; in fact, if this substrate of reality did not exist, there would be no physical world at all. It is in a sense—and perhaps in actuality—the "quantum vacuum" out of which the world is born anew moment to moment.

Moving to the second postulate of Huxley's working hypothesis, the physical world is not ultimately separate from its transcendental foundation, and so the perennial philosophy is a non-dualistic view of reality. There is no barrier between the so-called physical and metaphysical dimensions of reality (i.e., between the universe and its transcendent source); the two are a Oneness rather than a duality, and this is in contrast to systems of philosophy or religion that place a firewall between the transcendent realm and the physical world. For Perennialists, the universe arises from the Ground of Being, or, put the other way round, the Ground of Being takes form as the world around us. The One becomes the many, just as one ocean can rise up into multiple waves. Furthermore, and because we too are "waves" on the surface of a cosmic sea, our physical selves also arise from the Ground of Being. The Ground, therefore, is not only the Ground of Being but, consequently, the ground of our being as well.

The third postulate of Huxley's minimum hypothesis is that human beings have the latent ability to grasp the content of the two previous postulates experientially. That is, we have a capacity, whether we cultivate it or not, to go beyond intellectual descriptions of the Ground of Being (transcendent) and the Oneness of Being (immanent) to the direct experience of these realities, as did the mystics of the past—and as do some mystics today. While experiencing that aspect of ourselves beyond our bodies and minds, we come to realize that our essence is ultimately synonymous with *the* Essence, and so we feel a kinship with all reality arising from our shared oneness in the Ground of Being—that is, we, in our form as "waves," referencing the ocean analogy, come to *know* ourselves individually as one with the ocean itself and therefore intimately related to each other. This is what Huxley described as the "unitive knowledge" and mystics proclaim has true epistemic value.

Lastly, Perennialists generally believe that achieving such an awakening—via an upgrade in our state of consciousness—is the end and purpose toward which all human life aspires. Some Perennialists believe this is a step in our evolution mandated by nature, a goal inherent not only to our psyches but in the universe itself, while others conceive of it more modestly as simply the fulfillment of a latent human potentiality, albeit one that brings inner peace and great compassion. However, all Perennialists agree that the ultimate goal of our personal life, whether we realize it or not, is to wake up from our partial view of what is happening to us. In the awakened state, we have a richer vantage point from which to assess our lives, including the nature of our relationships with others (and remember that deciding how to treat these *others* is inescapable). This therapeutic aspect of waking up into our oneness with Being at a cosmic scale, is what Huston Smith was referring to in the quote that began this chapter: That "every emptiness we feel is Being eclipsed; all restlessness a flailing for the Being that we need; all joy the evidence of Being found." We are missing an awareness of the most fundamental aspect of what we are, confusing ourselves for skin-encapsulated egos that are isolated from each other and the natural world. But when the light outside floods into the Plato's Cave of our consciousness, we experience a profound sense of meaning and purpose, based on a richer apprehension of our place in the world.

This is the perennial philosophy in a nutshell. The majority of Perennialists today envision the unitive mystical experience as the most valuable form of mystical experience because it triggers an ontological insight into the nature of our being that we cannot ignore when forming our decisions about life's meaning, purpose and responsibility. There are other sorts of mystical experiences—if we define the term broadly enough to include, for instance, *psi* phenomena, near death experiences (which, by the way, sometimes also include unitive experiences), or entity encounters—but the apprehension of our interconnectedness with all creation (what some have termed our "inter-being" with all life), based on our mutual arising from the Ground of Being, is for them the apex of insight.

Without denying that other mystical experiences exist or have value, Perennialists hold that these other experiences generate less comprehension of what is really going on than the UME because they afford less perspective on our overall nature and situation. The unitive knowledge delivers something like what astronauts call the "overview effect" (experienced when they view the earth from space), setting our place in the world into a broader and more wholistic perspective. Again, this is the central premise of the perennial philosophy, and having looked briefly at what the perennial philosophy is, let me add a few words about what it *isn't*.

First of all, it isn't a religion. There is no church to join and no doctrine to follow, nor is there any set of rituals or practices that must be undertaken. Though some Perennialists—for instance, Fritjof Schuon and Rene Guenon, founders of the "traditionalist" school of perennialism—have been quite dogmatic about their particular interpretation of the unitive mystical experience, the majority of Perennialists hold their views more lightly. Huxley, for example, once argued that the greatest invention to emerge from the Scientific Revolution was not the steam engine or the reliable clock (used to coordinate the actions of the labor force), but the notion of a working hypothesis. Prior to the Renaissance, most people found meaning in the received knowledge of their church, temple, mosque, or synagogue, and that knowledge was presented to them as an immutable dogma to be followed without question. However, Huxley felt even spiritual truths—at least conceptual approximates of those truths—must be held provisionally.

Huxley also believed that the deepest truth is experiential, and therefore not contained by concepts, and that conceptual approximates will come closer to conveying that truth only if they're kept open to scrutiny and modification. Consequently, as I've already mentioned, there is generally no dogma or faith claim in the perennial philosophy. The goal is to attain the direct experience of your oneness with reality, not to memorize or have faith in any particular set of ideas about that oneness. Like the experiences of love and beauty, the UMF has an inherent value that is self validating and requires no settled interpretation. When I'm at a concert with my wife and we're grinning like idiots because the music is amazing, I don't need an explanation for why it's amazing; I simply *know*—I grok it directly. Its truth requires no theory. Likewise, the experience of noetic awakening, which is likely a close cousin of aesthetic experience, does not depend upon a settled opinion about its nature. In fact, its nature seems to defy settled opinion, so dogmas insult it. In fact, Huxley, Grof, Watts and others have argued that dogmatic interpretations of the UME have arisen mainly as attempts to claim intellectual sovereignty over the UME, which for them was a form of idolatry, claiming as Sacred something less than the Sacred.

Perennialists are also not religious in the sense that they advocate a form of *universalism*, as do Unitarians or Baha'is, not that those groups are somehow invalid. Neither Huxley, Smith, Grof, Vaughan, Watts, or Dass has argued that the perennial philosophy is the core position of the historical religions or, to put it another way, that all religions are really saying the same thing, which, of course, *would be* a form of universalism. Huxley was simply offering a theory about a discernible thread of experience across the world's mystical traditions, while acknowledging that the religions make disparate claims about the nature of that experience (if they even include it) and the nature of reality itself. (For instance, Buddhists don't believe in a Creator God while faith in a Creator God is central to Christianity and Islam. So how could we say these religions are saying the same thing?) Consequently, Huxley became upset when his editor tried—in 1945—to promote his book, *The Perennial Philosophy,* as the basis for a new religion, demanding the editor remove such language from the back cover. Again, Huxley was arguing there is a thread that reaches across many of the mystical traditions, not that this pattern is what matters *most* in each and every religion. The religions themselves should decide what is their core, what they value most and least. In some religions, like Vedantic Hinduism or Sufi Islam, the UME seems to be an essential focus, but in traditional Judaism and Christianity it is not. In summary, the perennial philosophy offers a mix of theories about a particular type of mystical experience, the UME, not a universalist religion or a unified theory of religion itself (more on this in the "Religion" chapter of Part III).

Moving along now, the perennial philosophy is also not a philosophy in the usual sense of the term. The Greek word *philosophia* means "love of wisdom" and Perennialists are most certainly lovers of wisdom, but their philosophical writings are mainly attempts to describe an experiential truth, not closed systems of thought based on rational speculation. Where philosophers, in modern times, have theorized over the nature of reality, Perennialists seek to access reality *directly,* later describing the experience as best they can. Huxley wasn't seeking to draft a systematic philosophy built up from logical axioms; he was trying to describe a shared interpretation of a shared journey into the world beyond Plato's Cave. What was it that the mystics said about the nature of reality beyond the shadow play? What did their enlightenment convey to them? This was the philosophy Huxley sought to describe.

Related to the above, one aspect of the Perennialist position on philosophy that always appealed to me is that it maintains we need not know everything in order to know enough. What I mean is that whether or not philosophers in the traditional sense ever succeed in drafting a definitive description of reality and our place in it, the truth of life may be available to us now in the UME. The UME doesn't rely upon descriptions of it to deliver the goods on our meaning and purpose; we know them directly via the experience. That's what I mean by "enough." If it were necessary for us to understand the universe completely in order to live fulfilled lives, then none of us ever has been or perhaps ever will be fulfilled. Jesus had no knowledge of quantum physics and the Buddha couldn't describe the human genome, but tradition tells us they knew what they needed to know—and what we need to know. Using science, we can explore the quantifiable universe in its complexity, and the application of what we learn may have great value (if we apply it properly, with the broader range of vision), but the mystics of the past have advised that we also should know the root of our being held in common with all life. That is what will provide us with the deepest sense of meaning and purpose, and therefore the deepest context for applying what we discover and create with the methods of science. Summing up the Perennialist position on systematic philosophy, the mystics realized long ago that in order to truly think outside the box, one must realize that sometimes thinking *is* the box, expanded experience being the higher necessity.

Having said that concepts have limitations, and having described the awakened state as a deep noetic apprehension of our oneness with reality, can we get a glimpse of what that experience might be like? Definitely. Mystics have related personal accounts of the experience in glowing prose and poetry, so we have what I term "prisoner reports" from those who've made it out of the Cave. It's an experience of deep interconnection with reality, and beyond that, even the sense that reality is looking out through our own eyeballs. To put some meat on the bones of this description, let me share a couple of firsthand reports—chosen from the internet rather than the traditional accounts to make clear that we're not talking about a phenomenon of expanded consciousness that only happened long ago. These quotes function not only as a preview of what's to come in the next chapter but, with a bit of effort on our part, what may come into our own lives:

Prisoner report 1 (offered by a woman):

Enlightenment is like, you were asleep and you wake up, where once you saw through a fog, now you see clearly. You don't have all the answers, but you no longer have questions. Where once you felt a void or empty, you now are full. Once you were lost, now you are found. Enlightenment is not a becoming, but a returning to. It is not something you gained, but something you realized. Enlightenment is like being alone in a world of many, now being all in One.

Prisoner report 2 (offered by a man):

It was something I didn't know that I could experience. I had no context or preparation for it. When I stopped—physically—to experience it, there was the most intense and simple and beautiful awe-inspiring nothing. It was beyond silent and peaceful. It was a calm bliss. It was Nothing. To give that Nothing qualities takes away from how Nothing it was. Silent, but that implies noise not being there, it was absolute nothing. It was a cocoon of a void and I was that void. But instantly it was also everything. I was everything, connected and a part of the whole and also the whole of the whole. I was complete and safe and home and felt total love and understanding. It was the key defining moment of my life, but also simple, pure and unremarkable, and that was the stunning thing, that it was so comfortable and natural. I glimpsed something. My key thoughts were of infinity and *everything is nothing. Nothing is everything.* It was 100% positive and I felt like I'd been let into a secret that wasn't hidden, that had been in plain sight the whole time. I just hadn't known how to see it, even though I had seen it and said it and known about it. This was an integrated experience of being it, One, nothing, everything, infinity—no time or place just all and nothing. It makes me smile now because I can't describe it well enough to convey the simplicity, intensity, intense simplicity. Eternal Communion. Certainty. Feeling the shape of the universe even as I was eating a sandwich and going to the launderette.

If the unitive mystical experience conveys a sense of oneness with reality, what does that imply about our own nature? In the next chapter we'll discuss more fully what you and I actually *are*.

PART TWO

Looking Deeper

4

WHO ARE WE?

"We are here today, tomorrow we are gone; mere shadows in a cosmic dream. But behind the unreality of these fleeting pictures is the immortal reality of Spirit."

Paramahansa Yogananda

"The soul's answer to the problem of time is the experience of timeless being."

Jacob Needleman

Since the beginning of human existence, we have wondered about our nature and our place in the universe. Consequently, every religion and philosophy that has ever existed has had an opinion on that matter. For instance, some say we are the "Crown of Creation" and should have dominion over all other species; some say we are simply another species within the circle of life; and still others contend that we are merely sojourners in an indifferent universe. And though these views disagree, they are all generated by the same question and the same desire for answers.

Significantly, something else that religion and philosophy often (but not always) have in common is the idea that we are victims of a predicament, and that we would be happier, or at least more content, if we could somehow transcend the mess we're in. For example, Taoists believe we would be happier if we came into harmony with nature; Christians believe we suffer because we have sinned against God's will; Buddhists think we suffer because our minds are controlled by our negative emotions; and Marxists hold that we suffer because we don't live in a classless society. In most cases, religions and philosophies (including the contents of this book) are given out as solutions to whatever human predicament they describe—that is, they are medicines for curing the *status quo*.

Speaking in these terms, the perennial philosophy shares something in common with Hinduism, Buddhism, Kabbala, and Greek mystical traditions in that when we deal with the root of our problem as a species, it's not that we're fundamentally flawed but that our flawed actions are the by-products of our wrong understanding of who we *really* are. Fundamentally, it's ignorance about our own nature that has caused our suffering—including our tendency to cause suffering for others. So then, who are we? Socrates advised that we should find out.

The perennial philosophy holds that we are composite entities made up of two primary aspects: a *relative aspect* that is bound in time and space and an *absolute aspect* that transcends time and space. The relative aspect is what we commonly refer to when we talk about who we are. It is our body and our mind, made up of our physical self and its thoughts, memories, emotions, gender and personality. Since these things are subject to time and space, the *body-mind*, as we'll call it, is temporary, individual and changeable (hence "relative"). It's the "street level" of our self. However, Perennialists theorize there is another aspect of our self that reaches into the metaphysical aspect of existence itself.

This aspect is not bound by the relative limits of the body-mind. In fact, it was never born and it will never die. In Hinduism, this deeper, more fundamental aspect is termed the *Atman*, the higher "Self" (capitalized here to indicate its absolute nature), and Hindus believe the need to experience it is what drives us to take rebirth lifetime after lifetime; we long to know our full nature and cannot rest until we have transcended our *avidya* or "ignorance" in that regard. We keep reincarnating like a kid staying back in school, never moving on until he or she gets their lessons right. And when we do get our lessons right, we stop coming back. Not all Perennialists believe in reincarnation, nor is it important to the position that they do, but all Perennialists believe experiential ignorance of our true Self—or, using another term (since many Perennialists don't describe it as a *self*), the absolute aspect of our being—is what keeps us back from our deepest happiness and highest insight.

Having said that, why don't we have an awareness of this transcendent aspect from the moment we're born? Why are we blind to all that we are in the first place? In answering this question, let's begin by noting that at birth we have no knowledge of *any* aspect of who we are, including the body-mind, and it's only over time that any level of our existence becomes revealed. Related to this, unfortunately, is the fact that as we gain information and insight about who we are, our inclination is to lock down on the body-mind as the whole story of our nature, distracting us from discerning the deeper levels of our being.

To make this clearer, imagine that you've never seen a movie and don't understand how movies are projected onto a movie screen. One day you enter a theater, arriving after the show has already begun. Suddenly out of nowhere, a mystic of some sort sits down beside you and whispers in your ear, "Do you see all that color, motion and change?"

You turn toward her and answer, "Of course, that's why I came. It's all part of the movie."

And the mystic, busy arranging her popcorn, replies, "Yes, but not the only part. There is a quieter part. Do you realize that right now, underlying all that color, motion and change, there is a pure white screen?"

You lean forward in your seat for a better look and then respond, "Nope, you're wrong. There's no white screen. There's only the movie."

The mystic chuckles, "I know you can't see it, but it's there. In fact, without the screen there could be no movie."

"Then why can't I see it?" you ask, thinking you've stumped her.

"Because it is being overwhelmed by the machine that is projecting those images onto it," the mystic explains. "The movie is obscuring the screen, even though the screen is necessary for the movie."

You consider this and ask, "Then how can I know if the screen is really there if I can't see it?"

"Ah," the mystic answers, "Good question!"

The mystic gets ready to share her method for experiencing the movie screen, which shouldn't be interpreted in this analogy to mean that the Absolute Self is a *tabula rasa* or a "blank screen" without content; it's actually an effulgence of content. But we'll leave her, the mystic, for the moment so we can stay on track with our explanation of the two levels of our being.

Perennialists write that in the same way the movie screen is overwhelmed by the movie, the deepest aspect of our being is overwhelmed by the mind's thoughts and emotions. Our five senses pull so much information into our daily experience as body-minds that we have become wrapped up in the drama of our "movie" such that we have considered it the whole story of our lives. Consequently, we find ourselves living only half a life, fixated on the activities of the body-mind but without the overview perspective on that experience gained when we know the "movie screen" aspect of what we are.

Related to this, some people, even while in ignorance of what's really going on, have intuitions of their absolute nature, and feel a longing to experience it—even when they can't put their finger on why. In the mystical traditions, this is a signpost of spiritual growth, for it indicates a degree of awakening has already occurred. Such people sense there is more to who they are than what they now grasp, and so they long to push the curtain aside and know themselves fully, as Socrates once said they should. Thus, they often become spiritual seekers, and if you're reading this book, you're likely to be among them. Perennialists generally believe that ignorance of who we are is the fundamental human predicament, giving rise to most of our psychological and social turmoil. Furthermore, Perennialists believe intuitions about the absolute aspect of self are responsible for the psychological tendency to think we're more than we appear to be, a pattern currently showing up in popular culture as the desire to become super-powered mutants or, referencing the Harry Potter books, magical wizards and witches rather than "muggles."

Of course, the deepest aspect of our being can be difficult to know, and even Socrates, who presumably spent a great deal of time with himself, seems to have found his nature to be a head scratcher. Having said this, most people take who they are for granted and are stumped by those who find themselves a mystery. Their experience of life as a body-mind is so thoroughly compelling they assume it defines the limits of who they are. They are a "plumber" or a "carpenter" or a "college professor" or a "house husband." However,

Perennialists believe Oscar Wilde was right to say, "Only shallow people truly know themselves." The rest must question and search, not taking for granted what others find obvious.

This reminds me of a story about the confusion that sometimes arises when people from both sides of the great divide (of "It's obvious who I am" vs. "I'm a mystery") meet. Several years ago, my good friend Charlie, who, like me, teaches philosophy, was knocked unconscious when a woman opened her car door in front of him as he passed by on his bicycle. Charlie was thrown over the handlebars and landed hard on the pavement, hitting his head. When he woke up in the hospital, a male doctor was shining a light in his eyes and looking for signs of concussion. "Do you know who you are?" the doctor asked. Charlie tried to focus his eyes, replying after a moment's hesitation, "No, but it's a very good question." Sometime later, after an hour or so, Charlie's daughter, Aletheia, arrived in his room, and the physician quickly pulled her into the hall for a private consultation. Showing deep concern, he explained that Charlie's condition was serious. Aletheia asked, "What makes you think so"? The doctor replied, "He doesn't even know who he is." Aletheia began to sob, but when the doctor explained what Charlie had actually said, her tears turned to laughter. "No, no, no!" she exclaimed as they reentered Charlie's room. "My dad is a philosophy professor. Get it? He's always like that! It just means he's being himself." Aletheia knew that even after a serious accident, her father, a true philosopher, remained curious about who he *really* was.

Backing up for a moment to deal with what keeps us in ignorance of all that we are, Buddhists argue that as we grow up (and, for them, also as we live from lifetime to lifetime), we develop habits that generate our conditioned response to the world. For the sake of our daily survival, we have formed patterns of behavior that we believe work for us, and once these patterns are established, we mostly operate on autopilot, going through the motions of our daily lives robotically to save time and energy. We get up in the morning, take a shower, get dressed, make breakfast, and commute to work, often without actually realizing we've performed these tasks.

I'm reminded of a time when, many years ago, I was walking my two daughters to school. My daughters, Sophie and Emma, were eight and six at the time and we were walking on a bright spring day, five blocks from home. As we reached an intersection, Sophie pointed out some beautiful tulips blooming in a yard down the street to our left. "Look dad!" she said. "Can we go this way to see the flowers?" I was lost in thought at the moment, though I agreed the red and yellow tulips were amazing, but then I answered, pointing out that the way we were going was quicker. "Are we in a hurry?" Sophie asked, with her sister also wondering what my point was. Thinking for a moment, I realized I had been running entirely on robot mind. I'm an American and Americans are always in a hurry! It's part of our national *consensus trance*, so my default mode was to rush the kids to school. But now, thanks to Sophie's curiosity, I realized we had no need to hurry. We could go any way we liked, literally and figuratively, enjoying the flowers at our leisure.

Operating on what psychologists term *automatization* or *habituation* can be useful in that we keep a reserve of energy for possible emergencies that might spring up, but this default mode of operations also creates a torpor state of consciousness in which we are pulled under the influence of habits related to what Buddhists term the *kleshas* or "afflictive emotions." Without the perspective that comes from expanded awareness of the deeper aspects of our being, the robotic and shadow aspects of our psyche can, as a friend of mine puts it, "rule the mainframe." For instance, a strong influence of desire may cause us to lust after consumer goods, and each trip to the mall brings us a small pay-off of happiness but the reflex of desiring has become so habitual, the avarice so deeply engrained, that the urge to own things rises in us without end, no matter how much stuff we accumulate. We get caught in a vicious cycle of owning and wanting to own, rarely lifting our heads up to ask whether or not all this shopping is adding up to anything. We become a kind of zombie or high-functioning sleepwalker, perpetuating our behavior without questioning whether or not it's fulfilling us—and sometimes knowing it's not, but continuing to do so anyway for lack of a perceived alternative.

According to the mystical literature, what we are ultimately trying to acquire is the experience of our deepest nature, the absolute aspect of our being, and only the possession of *that* (given its infinite nature) will satisfy us infinitely; that is, in a way that no other knowledge or consumer object can. Consequently, this is why mystics have been considered so valuable in traditional cultures. They remind us of the treasure that is always within us but that we overlook—or are distracted from—daily, like the invisible movie screen in the analogy used earlier, overwhelmed by the movie of our daily life.

In the same way that some people have an extraordinary talent for music or art, mystics are those who have a gift for non-ordinary states of consciousness, including the experience of unity with all reality. William Blake, Walt Whitman, Anandamayi Ma, and Kahlil Gibran were definitely such people of the past. However, Perennialists believe all of us have some noetic ability, given that we too have that deepest aspect of our being. Mystics help us develop our awareness of this by calling our attention to the benefits of knowing it. This is, in fact, why mystical literature and poetry are so deeply valuable; they point the way, helping to awaken a sensitivity within us toward what we're really seeking.

I've often heard my college students say they've never had a mystical experience or any kind of noetic opening, but when I ask them if they've ever had a "touchstone experience, pregnant with meaning" that keeps coming back to them even if they can't explain why, they often respond with comments like, "Well, I was on top of a mountain once and felt this tremendous sense of expansion that has stayed with me;" or "I was walking on the beach one morning with my dog and as the sun came up I started crying and felt like there was no past or future, only this wonderful *now*, and I just wanted to stay in that now forever;" or "I was in the middle of New York City one afternoon and suddenly everything shifted; whenever I made eye contact with someone I felt like I knew them deeply and we were somehow connected, though we were complete strangers." These, whether recognized or not, are mystical experiences. Specifically, in Perennialist terms, because in these moments when the world seems boundless and timeless, the experiencer is actually experiencing the timeless and boundless aspect of their own nature. Circumstances were such for these students that the Ground of Being or "movie screen" aspect of their being loomed into their awareness, giving them a moment of perspective on their everyday "movie." The trick, of course, is to find ways of making that insight happen more often. Furthermore, when such experiences happen more often, the relative aspect of self knows the absolute aspect more intimately, allowing the individual to make choices based on a richer understanding of their nature and circumstances.

Some readers may ask, "But what about the Buddhist concept of *anatman* ("no-self") and the claim that there is no *Atman* or absolute aspect of Self?" Does what I've said imply that Buddhist mystics can't agree with the perennial philosophy?

For Buddhists, our highest awakening comes when we realize we have no permanent self—on any level, absolute or relative. They believe the desire for a permanent self is what causes us to make our body-minds so precious, which is the root cause of egotistical behavior and fear of death. We must learn to accept, they argue, that the body-mind is not only impermanent but that our personality is little more than a collection of psychological and emotional habits. Furthermore, the movie screen, at least as an independent *self*, is also an illusion. For Buddhists, the absolute dimension of our being (and Mahayana Buddhists *do* believe in that dimension) is not us. The transcendental *dharmadatu or tathagatagarbha* aspect of reality (analogous to the Ground of Being) is absolute and unchanging, and we can experience it, but it has no personality and is not our private property. Consequently, it is not analogous to the Christian or Muslim concept of soul, given that souls are discrete entities that have the personalities of the body-minds they travel around with in life (and so, for instance, in heaven I would be a non-corporeal version of myself here on Earth). For Buddhists, the transcendent or metaphysical aspect of our existence, of all existence, is beyond any concept of an independent or permanent self (which is why a Buddhist friend of mine has a bumper sticker on her car that reads, "Honk if you don't exist!"). But Buddhist mystics, at least of the Mahayana variety, are still in general agreement with Perennialists on the issue of the deepest aspect of our being, and we'll see more clearly why when we discuss our next question: "Where are we?"

5

WHERE ARE WE?

"You are rather a sort of nerve-ending through which the universe is taking a peek at itself, which is why, deep down inside, almost everyone has a vague sense of eternity."

Alan Watts

Native Americans call this world the Great Turtle Island. Hindus call it Jambudvipa or *samsara,* the place where all creatures live and take rebirth. Science tells us that we're on the third planet from a minor star in a vast galaxy that is only one of billions of galaxies. Science also tells us that we live in a liminal zone between *quanta* (things) that get infinitely larger than us (planets, galaxies, etc.) and things that get infinitely smaller than us (molecules, atoms, quarks, etc). Humans have always scratched their heads over where we are. What is this place where we find ourselves? How is the cosmos actually configured? How big is it? How much of it can we know or comprehend? And what is our relationship to it—whatever the hell *it* is?

One place to start our inquiry is by saying that the perennial philosophy, in most of its iterations, never contradicts scientific facts (though it may refute certain theories), and so it is in agreement that we are on a planet orbiting a sun that is two-thirds of the way out from the center of the spiral galaxy we call the Milky Way—in a universe that is not only large but perhaps multi-dimensional. However, this is just part of the story, and not the most important part in terms of human experience and human happiness. Perennialists believe there are other aspects of the universe that bear upon our situation with an even greater significance than its size. And these aspects, closer to home (in fact, within us), influence our perceived connections to the natural environment.

In the academic discipline of philosophy there is a sub-discipline called ontology, which, derived from the Greek, is the *ology* ("explanation" or "study") of *onto* ("being" or "existence"). This is the area of philosophical inquiry dealing with what *truly* exists. What is real and what is illusion? If my friend, with whom—let's say—I'm sitting on a park bench, asks me to consider, "Do you think this is really happening to us or are we dreaming it?"—he or she is thinking as an ontologist. Or if you're a college student and your roommate, who has become thoughtful, asks you to consider if your life is *real* or if, "We might just be thoughts inside the mind of some giant alien who is dreaming both of us"—then they too are thinking ontologically.

In western ontology, since before the time of Socrates, there were thought to be two primary realms of existence: the *physical* and the *metaphysical* (note these terms themselves are derived from Greek). The sciences dealt with the physical world, since it's comprised of *quanta* or "materials" (at least seemingly so on our scale of existence) that can be weighed and measured, and the metaphysical world (or metaphysical *aspect* of the world), because it is literally "beyond the physical," could only be investigated with the mind or spirit, i.e., *noetically* (from the Greek word *nous,* meaning "mind" or "spirit"). For Plato, it was the influence of the metaphysical dimension that registers upon us as the ultimate compass and guide for judging what in life is "Good," "Beautiful," and "True." It was the source of all light outside of Plato's Cave, and as such revealed the deepest foundation for all *qualia* decisions—for instance, decisions related to human values, ethics, and tastes in art and music.

Just as we have discussed that there are two primary aspects of our nature, the body-mind (physical) and absolute aspect of self (metaphysical), Perennialists believe the universe also has two aspects. Underlying the universe (and all possible universes) is the same Ground of Being mentioned in the first postulate of Huxley's "Minimum Working Hypothesis" (chapter 3). Below the level of matter as we commonly experience it is the molecular level, and below that are the atomic and sub-atomic layers; however, even deeper than these is that substrate of reality that has no mass or dimension whatsoever.

Hindus have termed this foundation or Ground of Being *Brahman*; the Chinese have called it the "Nameless Tao;" Mahayana Buddhists refer to it as the *dharmadatu*; and Christians have called it the "Godhead." Emerson described it as the "Oversoul" or "World Soul;" William James referred to it as the "Mother-sea of consciousness;" Martin Buber, the Jewish theologian, called it the "Eternal Thou;" and Kabbalists refer to it as the *ein sof.* Myriad mystics from a wide range of times and places have given some name to that aspect of reality only discernible with the inner eye. This is the movie screen level of existence behind the whole story of where we are, not just in our individual lives but the story of the universe *en toto*. In summary, the Ground of Being is to the physical universe what our *deepest aspect of being* is to our body-minds, the metaphysical substrate upon which the physical layers of existence depend.

Exploring this further, the dichotomy between the physical and metaphysical is misleading in some sense because, as is stated in Huxley's second postulate, reality is not dualistic in its ultimate nature. The two aspects of reality have no firewall between them because the physical world is actually lifting up out of its metaphysical substrate—again, like waves lifting out of an expansive ocean. Put another way, the physical world is a *variegated manifestation of a singular phenomenon.* Let's unpack that for a moment. Just as the surface of an ocean displays myriad and seemingly separate waves that actually are not separate from the ocean itself, depending, as they do, on the ocean for their mutual existence, the physical world is really only the most manifest aspect of a seamless reality arising from its metaphysical foundation.

Turning to Hinduism again, I've said that their mystics call this Ground of Being *Brahman* but more specifically they call it *nirguna* Brahman, that is, Brahman "without characteristics," in contrast to *saguna* Brahman which for them is Brahman "with characteristics." Both levels of reality—physical and metaphysical—are equally "Brahman." Likewise, Perennialists describe reality as a oneness in which its physical and metaphysical aspects are not separate. Even our bodies are not truly separate from the deepest level of our being, but rather the most manifest or concrete aspect of what we are, the bleeding edge of our spirit. And here we stumble into a very interesting premise of the perennial philosophy, for even as our deepest aspect is not ultimately separate from our body-minds, it is also not perfectly separate from the deepest aspect of anyone else—or even of any *thing* else.

Our bodies are temporal arisings in the vast ocean of Being, but, as we've discussed, at our root we all have an absolute aspect that doesn't arise, nor does it fall away at death. Building off this idea, *the root of our being is non-different from the Ground or root of ALL being.* In other words, your ultimate aspect, my ultimate aspect, and the universe's ultimate aspect are, ontologically speaking, a Oneness. Nothing—not even a God or Goddess—escapes it. And this is why the Christian mystic Meister Eckhart once wrote: "To gauge the soul we must gauge it with God, for the Ground of God and the Ground of the Soul are one and the same." The upshot of this is that there is ultimately no separation between what you are and what I am; my eternal essence and your eternal essence are part of the same metaphysical Ground, which is why Ralph Waldo Emerson often spoke of reality's foundation as the "Over Soul;" it is a single living consciousness looking out through all sets of eyes—from people to porpoises, from birds to bison—and with nothing separate from it.

Let me tell a quick story. People often scratch their heads at the seemingly enigmatic claims of mystics, but if you've understood what I've just said, the upshot of many of those claims becomes clear. Several decades ago there lived in Rishikesh, India, a Hindu pilgrimage center at the base of the Himalayas, a mystic named Tat Walla Baba. He kept his hair in long dreadlocks and only wore a small bit of white cloth around his waist for modesty's sake. One evening he sat cross-legged in the dirt, conversing with a group of English tourists. Delighting in his sense of humor, as well as his spiritual insights, an elderly woman commented, using a translator, "Oh Baba, you're so wonderful! Please say you'll come to London for a visit!"

After the translator passed along her request, the baba made a response that caused the translator to guffaw.

"What did he say?" the woman wondered.

"Well," the translator responded with a smile, "he says he *is* London!"

The woman was perplexed. However, Tat Walla Baba's inner Self evidently felt so expansive to him at that moment that he took it to be not only large but synonymous with the cosmos—including London.

Another illustration of this principle might be found in a *New Yorker* cartoon I once saw in which an old yogi sat in front of his Himalayan cave with a young boy. While gesturing to the high mountains all around them, the yogi remarked, "Son, someday all of this will be *you*."

Since we're now considering the Perennialists' view of the universe and our place in it, there's one more detail worth mentioning, which deals with a consequence of considering the Ground of Being as the World's "Soul." The premise seems to imply there are no separate souls as Christians or Muslims think of them, and some Perennialists believe that's actually true, but others disagree. For example, it's common to find one or other Perennialist theory that somehow includes—at least partially—the idea of a personal consciousness that survives death.

To make this point clear, let's start by asking some questions. First—When we die, are all of our personality and individuality dissolved into the World Soul, just as waves are subsumed into the ocean when the wind subsides? Or is some aspect of our relative individuality retained after death? Different Perennialists have different opinions. All Perennialists believe in the Ground of Being as the World Soul, but they differ on whether or not there are also individual souls. Some believe all individuality is lost at death but offer that, "Why should we care? What is lost when the river meets the sea? Water meets water. We lose our individuality, but already, before our death, we—if awakened—identify with the World Soul as what is most truly 'us,' and that never dies."

Other Perennialists believe the physical self has several layers, nested together like Russian dolls, and at the most subtle level of our individuality is the "causal body." This level of self survives the death of the outer body and is what may take rebirth in another fetus, continuing its quest for awakening. In this latter interpretation, the "causal body" (the *jiva* for Hindus and the *citta-santana* or "continuum mind" for Mahayana Buddhists) is like the SIM chip we used to have in our cell phones. The SIM chip, containing personal information—such as phone numbers and photos—could be removed from one phone and placed inside another after the "death" of a broken phone. That is, it could be transferred into a new "phone body" to retain all the data from its previous life. Similarly, there is, in some views, an aspect of the relative self that survives death and continues in other bodies.

Perennialists have a range of theories about the relationship between body-minds, individuated souls, and the Ground of Being/World Soul, including views of what happens to us at death. However, these theories take us beyond this introductory text. The job here is to lay out the core perspective of Perennialism, and we've now drafted that with reference to the nature of existence (both our own existence and that of the cosmos). We live in a universe that is vast and complex because it arises, nanosecond to nanosecond—that is, *right now*—out of its metaphysical foundation. And though we may, as body-minds, be as insignificant to this universe as individual waves are to an ocean, at the root of our being we *are* the ocean, and have the innate capacity to experience life from that perspective.

We've said the metaphysical substrate of the universe is without qualities, a Ground of Being that is beyond time and space. But what about the physical aspect of the universe? Or, if you will, what is the nature of the universe's "body-mind?" If you're curious, this topic is covered in the chapter on "Nature" in Part III, and this chapter can be read even in advance of the chapter that follows this one. You decide. But otherwise, let's turn to what is perhaps life's biggest question, which is "Where are we going?" Or put another way, "What is the meaning of life?"

6

WHERE ARE WE GOING?

"Silence is only as worthy as what we can bring back from it,
and what we can weave of it into the clamor of the world."

Pico Iyer

Everyone in the world has family and friends, and actions and objects, that matter to them. They have to feed their kids; they want a better place to live; they're worried that their daughter won't be allowed an education; they hope their son's health will improve; they want a loving relationship; they want a job that isn't too boring; they fear the river will rise and the dam will break, and so on. Some of their concerns are small ("Should I buy the blue sweater or the green one?") and some of them are life changing ("Can I reconcile with my spouse or should I leave this relationship?"), but in all cases, most of everyone's days are spent advancing the agenda of their various concerns.

Looking more closely into the daily actions of any individual, it's possible to distinguish which of their concerns take priority over the others. For instance, a young man in Panama loves to play soccer and spends most of his free time on the field, but his free time is limited because his wife and two young daughters are a higher priority. He loves soccer but he loves his family more, feeling a strong need to safeguard their welfare by going to work. And so there are hierarchies of concern in people's lives, including, for most individuals, and as we've discussed, an ultimate concern (UC) that takes precedence over all else. For one person that UC could be his or her family, like the man in Panama, and for another it might be the goal of achieving fame and fortune. In traditional cultures, there was, and is, a shared ultimate concern that forms the bedrock of all concerns, private and public. For Christians and Muslims, the UC that all interests line up behind is the priority of reaching heaven. In Judaism, the primary goal has been to establish a righteous "Kingdom of God" here on earth, with everyone following God's Law as it's set down in the Torah. Such UCs inform the decision-making process of these groups at both the collective and personal levels, setting the metrics for what should and should not be done on a daily basis.

How should I treat animals? Should I have premarital sex? Should I drink alcohol? Should gay marriage be legal? Does marriage even matter? Can I eat meat? Is capital punishment morally correct? The answers depend upon how these actions line up against the ultimate concern—however vaguely realized—that directs a person's life. If our Panamanian soccer player, for example, were an Orthodox Jew, his family must take precedence over his hobby, no matter how much he enjoys it, but even his family must be shunned if their actions contradict his ultimate concern of following God's Law. Consequently, Peter Berger, a sociologist of religion, has called the traditional ultimate concerns the "sacred canopies" of their respective religions, because they offer an umbrella of meaning and purpose that presides over actions at every level—in short, answering the question, "Where are we going?" in very specific terms.

Saying all this, we are about to look at the UC of the perennial philosophy, but just before we do, let's be clear that the highest goal of either a society or an individual need not be based on a traditional religion. Every worldview or ideology, whether religious or secular, has a UC that guides the behavior of those who embrace it. For example, Russian communists of the Soviet period prided themselves on having the world's least religious society, but that didn't mean their ideology had no direction. Their UC was to create a classless society based on scientific principles rather than "outdated superstitions," and they believed religion was counter-productive to that goal.

Scrutinizing the same issue on an individual level, a person might argue that they are not religious and have no UC of any kind, but as I explained in Chapter 1, that is not the case. If a person says, "I don't believe in ultimate concerns, so I have no goals and spend my days playing video games to kill time," they still haven't escaped a prioritization of concerns. They're simply saying, "I make having no UC a justification for my UC of playing video games." One way or another, everyone sets their moral compass and directs their behavior according to an ideology, whether or not that ideology is the outcome of careful thought, an unconscious inheritance from their parents and culture, or simply the accumulation of mental habits. In a nutshell, having a sloppy or sleepy ideology does not mean an ideology isn't present. As I said earlier, our actions (and inactions) in the world are expressions of our concerns, and concerns are inescapable, no matter how robotic or rudimentary they are in form.

Of course, it's also true that the issue of UCs is psychologically complex and people do not always live up to the ultimate concern they embrace. A person may want to be a good Muslim but finds that they enjoy a glass of wine from time to time, though alcohol is forbidden in Islam, or they may be a Marxist but find that certain "bourgeois" pleasures that are unassociated with the collective good (for instance, owning an expensive car) appeal to them. These "guilty pleasures," as we commonly call them, are pursuits that contradict a person's UC but are still tolerated, rationalized or repressed because they fulfill some lesser concern to which the person is also attracted. These divergent concerns and their relationship to the individual's UC form an entire field of psychology, revealing cases, for example, in which a certain person becomes overly neurotic due to the guilt of compromising their UC (a condition termed *cognitive dissonance*) or another in which someone becomes so dogmatically fixated on their UC that they can't see outside it, causing them to become a fanatic. But these psychological ramifications, though deeply interesting, transcend the purposes of this short book. Right now, it's time to outline the ultimate concern of the perennial philosophy.

Moving to the heart of the matter, the goal, as we've already discussed, is to WAKE UP, to directly experience the UME or "unitive knowledge." We must discover fully and experientially who and what we are, and this includes disentangling ourselves — at least temporarily — from the superficial identities that have accumulated on our psyche like barnacles on a ship. When, in the context of the body-mind, we know that we are more than just the body-mind, we achieve what Huxley identified as our "final end," the goal that all our other goals and aspirations have been leaning towards, consciously or unconsciously.

According to the biographies of renowned mystics, this spiritual break-through triggers a dramatic transfiguration. We realize we are more than what Alan Watts once termed "skin-encapsulated egos." In the past, we have confused the limits of our previous state of consciousness for the limits of consciousness itself, like a person who only watches one channel on their television set, day after day, not realizing other channels are available. In the awakened state, the World Soul becomes a living presence experienced by the body-mind as what Hindus term *sat-chit-ananda*, "truth-conscious-ness-bliss." For mystics of all traditions, the awakened state feels like it is inarguably real; it conveys the sense that all individual consciousnesses are subsets of an unbounded field of *Consciousness*; and, emotionally speaking, the attendant freedom from the limits of the body-mind that one feels registers as freedom and bliss.

In the awakened state, the individual achieves a liberation from igno-rance that reorients them in the world. As an individual, they continue to accept that they are only small specks in a complex and colossal cosmos, but on another level they experience themselves continuously as non-different from the source of the cosmos. Consequently, at their death, individuality may or may not be lost forever, but the pinch of death is set inside the per-spective that on the deepest level of their being they were never born and can never die. There is then less tendency to cling to the dying body, and without a need to cling to it, the psyche is able to surrender into the World Soul, the Godhead, the Ground. Consummate with this view, St. Catherine of Genoa once wrote: "My 'Me' is God, nor do I recognize any other Me except my God Himself." Her individuality had become totally subsumed into the cos-mic presence.

This *telos* or goal of reaching enlightenment relates to the individual but what about society? It may be joyful—and even fun—for a person to wake up like the Buddha but what about everybody else? What about the goals of society? Doesn't the perennial philosophy have a selfish Ultimate Concern? Isn't it too focused on individual happiness? Perennialists say no.

Perennialists point out that societies are fundamentally collections of individuals, and whatever fulfills all the individuals in a society must fulfill society itself. The quality of a society (e.g., in terms of intelligence, compassion, creativity, and happiness) is directly dependent upon the quality of the individuals who make it up. If the individuals in a village are kind, resourceful, loving and imaginative, that will likely result in—at the social level—less violence, less dogmatism and less tension. Conversely, if a community is made up of individuals who are angry, selfish and envious, what should we expect to find as a collective effect? Should we expect harmony and civility? Probably not. Using an analogy to summarize this point, a forest is only as green as the trees in the forest are green. If each individual tree (i.e., citizen) in the forest (i.e., society) is green, then the forest is also green. "Green-ness" cannot be mandated from the top down by politicians or tyrants (though good public policies can facilitate individual awakenings and that is to be acknowledged) and neither can kindness or creativity. But if each individual in a society strives to 'green' themselves by realizing all that they are, the benefits of that upgrade in consciousness will ripple out into their behavior, with the benefit for society growing organically. This is why Perennialists of all stripes contend that the unit of national and international peace is the 'inner peace' of individual citizens.

From this perspective, one goal of society should be to create circumstances and institutions that facilitate awakening, perhaps in ways that are similar to those of Scandinavian countries who currently safeguard the physical health and productivity of their communities by maximizing preventative healthcare at the individual level. Without being overly romantic (though it may sound so to cynics), such societies have existed many times in the past, and even today the Dalai Lama identifies spiritual enlightenment as the primary concern of his people and their institutions. Similarly, the Buddhist nation of Bhutan does not keep track of its GNP (Gross National Product) but carefully tracks its GNH, its "Gross National Happiness," by collecting responses to questionnaires issued annually to each citizen.

Taking this line of investigation one step further, wouldn't a focus on personal awakening largely result in an accumulation of selfish citizens—each sitting smugly in their own little bubble of bliss? And prior to their awakening aren't they also being socially irresponsible, perhaps sitting in Himalayan caves contemplating their navels?

Again, Perennialists say no, or at least, not necessarily (since individuals can indeed delude themselves). Someone might begin their particular practice for a selfish reason (e.g., "I'm going to get enlightened so people will think I'm cool!"), given that they are in ignorance of their true nature, but based on the testimony and behavior of mystics from the past, Perennialists argue that as people awaken and reorient themselves, their new outlook includes a premium placed on altruism.

The enlightened person remains self-interested, but who or what is the self that they are interested in? Now, with the World Soul looking out through the eyes of their body-minds (at least partially), some aspect of their concern has expanded to a cosmic proportion, even as their egotistical self-focus has dwindled. When the individual wakes up to their full nature, they experience the shared essence of all creation and the profound interconnectivity of all things, cultivating what Mahayana Buddhists call *bodhichitta*, literally the "mind of enlightenment" but glossed in their tradition as the "altruistic mind." Expanded consciousness results in expanded compassion, or put another way, as Aldous Huxley once remarked, "Kindness is applied mysticism."

How can we determine if someone has reached full awakening or Huxley's "final end?" We can gauge it by the degree of compassion they exhibit in their behavior. No compassion, no awakening. If they strut around seeking converts, disciples, and groupies (enacting the usual Ponzi scheme of spirituality, placing themselves at the top) or exclaim about how wonderfully enlightened they are, we can be sure they're still mired in ego and delusion.

Some gurus or teachers, even among those whose viewpoints are generally in agreement with the perennial philosophy, seem to have believed that whatever an enlightened person says or does is spontaneously correct on the moral level, due to the fact that they hold a cosmic perspective. Consequently, behavior that might be deemed anti-social becomes justified, by either them or their devotees, on the grounds that they are tearing down worn-out cultural conventions or shaking disciples out of their personal ignorance. However, these justifications are rarely more than that, justifications for selfish behavior, based more on ego than privileged insight. To give but three examples, the actions of such gurus as Swami Muktananda, Amrit Desai, and Fred Lenz have provided cautionary tales. So-called enlightenment is fine if it leads to kindness but otherwise it's a counterfeit, for even if the "kingdom of heaven lies within," it remains our duty to bring it out into the world.

Using the above metric, most Perennialists would agree that a Red Cross volunteer, or a member of Doctors without Borders, or a folk singer inciting social justice, is more useful to the world than an immoral or self-righteous guru claiming personal sovereignty over the Ground of Being. In summary, Huston Smith has written that, "Traits matter more than States," meaning that improved *traits* of behavior are more valuable than flashy *states* of consciousness. Furthermore, improved behavior is the litmus test for any supposed upgrades in awareness. In this regard, note that both the words *conscious* and *conscience* derive from the same Latin and Greek word *conscientia,* "consciousness." For the ancient Greeks especially, behavior becomes increasingly moral as consciousness expands, and for Perennialists, the former is also the ultimate test of the latter. As a brief addendum to this point, not all who reify mystical experience believe that 'higher states' necessarily lead to improved 'traits,' nor that they must for these noetic states to be important metaphysically, but, in general, Perennialists believe they should.

As a last word on the issue of "Where are we going?"—it's important to note that there are nuances in the ways Perennialists view the goal. For some, enlightenment is an innate evolutionary goal of the human psyche and we are destined by our very nature to seek and find it. For others, it is even the primary goal of the cosmos, with God or the universe consciously eager for us to wake up. In these instances, enlightenment is primary to the direction of human existence, often with humans holding a unique place among sentient beings, including animals. However, today we also find Perennialists who view the goal of awakening more humbly and provisionally.

These neo-perennialists (and these more humble sorts also come in different stripes) entertain the idea that enlightenment, though possible and entirely valuable, may only be a capacity we have developed as an interesting and accidental by-product of our biological evolution, like color vision or complex speech, with no ultimate or God-given import of any kind. For these Perennialists, we do not have a cosmic role in the universe, nor is the universe interested in our waking up. In their sense, enlightenment is a goal we might set for ourselves, as we might like to achieve better health or receive a college degree, but it is a self-directed and modest goal rather than a cosmic wish. Who is right? Again, there's no consensus. However, the good news, as we've said, is that we can hold any and all such perspectives provisionally—remaining undecided on the issue of conceptual frameworks while exploring all of them.

With this said, we now have a clear idea of the ultimate concern of the perennial philosophy, which is to achieve spiritual awakening. This brings with it a sense of personal meaning (based on fuller understanding of what we are) and social purpose (based on the realization that we share soul-space with those around us). If the reader wishes more information about this particular subject, skip ahead for a moment to the chapter on "Enlightenment" in Part III, but remember that the truth that liberates is not a set of ideas. One may understand and agree with the content of this book, or any book for that matter, but that doesn't constitute the highest insight for Perennialists. To achieve that goal, we must have the UME itself. And how can we do *that*? This brings us to the last chapter of our overview, which deals with the methods of waking up.

7

HOW DO WE GET THERE?

"Place yourself in the middle of the stream of power and wisdom which animates all whom it floats, and you are *without effort* impelled to truth, to *right*, and a perfect contentment."

Ralph Waldo Emerson

"Be your own authority. Determine for yourself what is true. Take responsibility for your actions and the quality of your life."

Rabbi Rami Shapiro

The goal of the perennial philosophy, as we've described it, is to break free from habituated patterns that keep us in a mental and spiritual torpor, while also waking up to that aspect of ourselves that transcends time and space. However, what is the means for reaching that goal? This, of course, is a critical issue because we don't only want to read about the UME, we want to *experience* it.

To begin, first it's important to note that though the methods for awakening are often referred to as "paths," we won't actually be going anywhere. There is no town or dimension of reality called enlightenment; instead, awakening is a state of consciousness in which this world is experienced as it fully is, though we've been unable to see it that way. Consequently, some adepts haven't needed a method for awakening and seem to have woken up spontaneously. The Indian mystic Jiddu Krishnamurti claimed this happened to him, and others have given similar accounts.

Some individuals appear to have a natural talent for mystical experience in the same way that others have a talent for music. It comes to them easily, unsolicited, and with little or no need for procedures like meditation, yoga, drumming or prayer. Raimon Panikkar, a mystic and scholar of religion, refers to this talent as the *capax dei,* literally, the "capacity for God." Teresa of Avila, the Catholic saint, had this aptitude from an early age, as, much more recently, did the Hindu female adept Anandamayi Ma. They were by nature savants of noetic sensitivity. But how about the rest of us? As with the talent for music, some of us have enormous gifts and some of us do not, but all of us have some trace of this ability, which is why we do, from time to time, stumble into an epiphany of our timelessness—for instance, while standing on top of a mountain or sitting by the sea. And this ability, however latent or meager, can be cultivated (by standing on top of a mountain, for instance). The trick is to find processes or methods that reliably trigger the experience of timelessness and unity for you.

The various mystical traditions have described specific paths that are believed useful for any serious seeker. And so we find Mevlevi *dervishes* whirling in place; Native American shamans entering sweat lodges; Carmelite nuns engaging in contemplative prayer; Zen monks focusing on their breath; Hindu swamis repeating Sanskrit mantras, and so on and so forth, each tradition with its own practices and expert guides. And given that these practices have proven somewhat reliable, a subset of Perennialists (called the "Traditionalists") recommend these methods exclusively, arguing that it's somewhat absurd, or at least unnecessary, to bushwhack our way up the mountain of expanded consciousness when there are already established trails in each religion. Furthermore, having a guide or teacher who knows the terrain and has a vetted reputation for leading novices can be useful. Would there have been a Swami Vivekananda without a Sri Ramakrishna to lead the way? Or a John of the Cross without a Teresa of Avila? Perhaps not.

Having said this, the majority of Perennialists believe it's not a one size fits all situation, and different people will be drawn to different paths, including paths from cultures other than their own. This is fine with the Traditionalists among the Perennialists, by the way, as long as the aspirant chooses from within the established religious traditions and then sticks with their choice. The assumption is that the various means are analogous to separate trails toward the unitive knowledge, different in their characteristics but leading to the same ultimate insight. In addition, the Traditionalists hold that there's no need to look beyond the established pathways because they already offer a variety of approaches, accommodating any personal proclivity. For example, Traditionalists believe that within Hinduism alone there are numerous practices that have stood the test of time. And, since I've referenced Hinduism, let's briefly explore their specific methods for getting there.

A common term for spiritual practice in Hinduism is *sadhana*, but equally common is *yoga*. In the West, this word is usually associated with stretching exercises, however, that type of yoga—*hatha yoga*—is just one of many. The word *yoga* derives from the Sanskrit verb root *yuj*, meaning "to unite," and refers to the conscious "union" of the everyday self with the Divine Ground of Being. For instance, in the first chapters of the *Bhagavad-Gita*, the Hindu god Krishna tells his pupil Arjuna that there are three primary "yogas" or methods for achieving union. The first is *jnana yoga*, a method in which one learns to distinguish the "real from the unreal" by separating the partial, distorted, conditioned, and sleepy orientation people usually have toward the world from the wholistic perspective of the awakened mind. In Hinduism, this path also involves meditation to quiet the mind of thoughts so that the deep Self can be revealed. Remembering our analogy of the movie screen from an earlier chapter, the idea here is that the best way for the mystic sitting in the theater (remember her?) to convince us there is a pure white screen beneath the movie is to turn off the projector. And likewise, if we wish to experience the movie screen underlying our particular movie, Hindus believe it's useful to turn off the projector of the thinking mind to reveal the presence of what lies beneath. However, getting beyond Hinduism, this path, the path of knowledge, is for Perennialists (as it was for Plato) a way to get outside the cave of shadows into the sunshine, whether we achieve that illumination via stopping the mind or not.

The second method or pathway Krishna recommends in the *Gita* is that of *karma yoga*, the path of altruistic action, and on that pathway we find those who, intentionally or unintentionally, expand their spiritual lives by sublimating their egos to the service of others. The primary question that moves karma yogis forward is not so much "Is this true?" but "Does this help?" In today's world, Peace Corp volunteers and Red Cross volunteers are two types of karma yogis, as are those who visit the sick or bake cookies for charity fundraisers.

Finally, Krishna outlines the method of *bhakti yoga*, the pathway of religious devotion. This is the path of prayer, ceremony, and pilgrimage, but according to Krishna, and the adepts of other religions, it is primarily a path of surrender to God, in whatever form. The guiding principle here is "Thy will be done," not "My will be done," and it has produced some of the greatest adepts of the mystical traditions, including St. Francis (though we must admit he also had *karma yoga* tendencies, given his service to the poor and infirm). For those on the path of devotion, the journey to awakening is a journey home to God. Via the route of selfless love, the aspirant finds their way back to their source as did the Prodigal Son to his father. This path of returning is brilliantly described in the poetry of Kabir, Teresa of Avila, Rumi, and Rabindranath Tagore.

One of the most interesting sections of Krishna's exposition in the *Gita* comes at the very end, in chapter 18, verse 63, and I mention it here because it has relevance regarding methods of awakening in the perennial philosophy. After Krishna has outlined the three yogas, Arjuna is curious to know which method works best and which he should choose; however, Krishna ends with a very telling comment: "Thus to you has been expounded the knowledge that is more secret than the secret; after considering it fully, you should act as you think best." At the end of the discourse, Krishna's answer is basically, "That's for you to decide." And here Krishna is recognizing that different pathways appeal to different personality types. Karma yoga, the yoga of "action," is not best suited for those who enjoy contemplation, and quiet meditation is unappealing to those who like to keep busy. Growth toward spiritual maturity is intensely personal, given that no matter how many mystics have woken up throughout history, this will be the first time *you* have woken up; consequently, personal choice, based on one's own nature, is deeply important when it comes to choosing a path.

What works for me may not work for you; in fact, my practice may distract you from what is most beneficial to your growth. Sitting meditation and monastic life may be excellent for one person but only a source of frustration for another. Regarding this, the fifteenth century Zen master Ikkyu often complained about growing up in a Buddhist monastery—he even wrote a poem titled, "I Hate the Smell of Incense," preferring to spend time hiking in the mountains to sitting in a meditation hall.

In strong contrast to the view of the Traditionalists, Aldous Huxley—along with Gerald Heard, Frederic Spiegelberg, Alan Watts, and other Perennialists of the past—believed the religious pathways are not exclusive methods for awakening but rather a set of road blocks preventing it. Huxley argued that these old pathways, replete with toll booths, tend to be contaminated with jealousy, entrenched thinking, and petty power structures. Priests and functionaries are drawn to power and control, Huxley believed, so they form hierarchies and don't appreciate wild mystics rolling around like loose cannons. In a nutshell, institutions breed gate-keepers rather than way-showers, so Huxley argued we're better off finding what works for ourselves. Here he extends Krishna's advice about personal choice beyond the religious pathways, even advocating the use of psychedelic drugs in the awakening process, at least if one has guidance for how to use them properly.

Huxley argued that too often those who take a traditional path become guilty of confusing a means for a goal. The goal is enlightenment and the *yogas* are simply a set of means for reaching it, but sometimes practitioners elevate their means to the status of an end-in-itself. They enshrine and sacralize their method, claiming their way is the best, that all other methods are foolhardy or profane, or that there is no salvation outside their tradition or interpretation of the UMF—but the profanity is their own, Huxley believed. They have taken something that is less than the Sacred (i.e., their religion, teacher, or pathway) and enshrined it *as* the Sacred, raising a relative means to the level of an absolute ends, which, by the way, was Huxley's specific definition of idolatry.

But who's right about all this? Is it Huxley's camp or the Traditionalist camp (including from the past Frithjof Schuon and Martin Lings and today Harry Oldmeadow and others)? The first thing to say here is that there's no uniform answer within Perennialism, given there's a range of positions, but my personal answer, at least for the context of this book, is "yes." What I mean to say is that I side with Krishna in terms of his recommendation about personal choice. If a traditional religious pathway calls to you and works for you, why avoid it? And if it doesn't work for you, why keep it? Why not try something different—whether a path from another tradition or something completely unorthodox? Perhaps you can even make your own tool box of approaches, mixing techniques as you find them useful. (My friend Mirabai Starr refers to this approach as "spiritual cross-training," adding that she is, by nature, "spiritually promiscuous!")

My personal iteration of the perennial philosophy, in terms of method, is situated somewhere between the "follow a tried and true approach" of the Traditionalists and the "go your own way" of Huxley, Heard, and Watts. My view is closer to that of Huston Smith, Mirabai Starr, and Ram Dass. I accept Huxley's adage that no path should be enshrined, but why denigrate any path, whether traditional, liberal, or conservative? Huston Smith often spoke of what he termed the "sin of particularity," which is the view that whenever someone claims their particular teacher or method is the best, they are implicitly wrong. There is no such thing as THE way or the BEST way; there are simply ways, and those are many. Huston is often counted among the Traditionalists, whose viewpoint he certainly respected, but as an open-minded college professor, he also encouraged students to explore methods beyond religion, even advising them to attend workshops at the Esalen Institute and other such venues. In brief, he supported everyone who wished to grow spiritually, even those for whom religion had no appeal.

Since the 1960s, we've seen the emergence of a wide range of new and sometimes revolutionary methods for triggering awakening, including Gestalt therapy, sensory deprivation tanks, biofeedback technologies, brain-entrainment devices, and psychedelic therapies. In addition, we've not only seen the western embrace of Asian methods like Zen meditation, Tai Chi, and yoga but also the re-awakening of pathways embraced by the nineteenth century Romantics. Today it's quite common to find practitioners who claim their spiritual practice involves spending time in nature, immersing themselves in the experience of art and music, or surrendering into the love of another person. The Romantics believed these were all doorways into the Sublime and walking through them led to spiritual and moral elevation. Many aspirants continue to believe the Romantics were right. But the question arises: are these radical or unconventional pathways viable?

I say yes in agreement with W.T. Stace, who, while teaching philosophy at Princeton, argued what he called the "principle of causal indifference," implying that if a technique works, then it works—whether, according to whichever expert's opinion, it *shouldn't* work. Stace pointed out, in *Philosophy and Mysticism* (1960), that the German mystic Jacob Boehme (1575-1624) claimed he had been catapulted into awakening by observing the reflection of the sun in a pewter bowl. Is looking into a pewter bowl a viable method for reaching enlightenment? Stace's position was: why not? The awakening is what matters, not the method for triggering it, and if awakening occurs, the method *must be viable*. In agreement with this view, William Richards, a contemporary researcher at Johns Hopkins and author of *Sacred Knowledge* (2017), makes the case that even psychedelic drugs can be useful triggers for the unitive mystical experience. Our Perennialist touchstones (Huxley, Smith, Vaughn, Grof, Watts, Dass), not to mention Native American groups who use peyote, psilocybin, and Ayahuasca as sacraments, all agreed with Richards' view.

Of course some methods may work better than others, and some methods may not be generally advisable. For instance, Teresa of Avila experienced many of her most powerful insights while suffering from life-threatening illness, but would we advise contracting a disease as a way to wake up? Meditation or Centering Prayer might be more prudent and reliable. Joseph Campbell, a ground-breaking Perennialist who studied the world's myths and found discernible patterns within them, recommended that you "follow your bliss." Find the path that has personal appeal for you, and once you're on it, pay attention to whether or not it's working. You'll know when you're getting somewhere because you'll find yourself opening not only to inner peace but also humility, gratitude, love, and kindness.

Like the experiences of art and music, glimpses of awakening are implicitly expansive and therapeutic. Moreover, aesthetic experiences are intimately related to mystical experiences, so for some people art and music are the actual pathway. Sufis, for example, use music and dance to remember God— or in their own parlance, to "re-member" or reconnect themselves experientially to God, merging into oneness. In summary, I agree with St. Teresa: "Do whatever best awakens you to love," and keep in mind that even the most mundane of daily chores can trigger upgrades in consciousness if performed with the right attitude and intention, which is why Zen practitioners often sing the praises of "chop wood, carry water." Our higher nature—or if you prefer, "the Invisible Sun Within Us"— is always present, if we only have eyes to see, and there are myriad ways to clear our vision.

You've now completed my overview of the perennial philosophy. But what does this viewpoint suggest about psychology and the nature of the human mind? How do works of art and music serve to trigger awakening? What does the perennial philosophy tell us about how we should interact with the natural environment? What about the existence of God, gods, and entity encounters? What about loving relationships? Who are the perennial philosophers today? These and other questions are addressed in Part III. At this point, having finished the overview, you are free to read whichever of the following chapters most appeal to you, shuffling them and reading them in whichever order you wish. However, once you're finished, I recommend reading the short "Epilogue" at the end—and you might also want to browse the appendix of "Further Reading."

PART THREE

Exploring Specific Topics

RELIGION

"When asked about the comfort of religion as a crutch, Huston Smith made a scowl and answered, 'I'm not seeking comfort in my religion. I'm looking for challenges to be my best in each moment of my existence.'"

Huston Smith, as related by Philip Goldberg

$\mathcal{W}$*e've already noted* that Perennialists collectively believe there is a mystical experience that arises in all cultures and has great value. It rises everywhere and always because it's implicit in the relationship between the human psyche (including its purely metaphysical aspect as the Ground of Being) and the natural world (including *its* purely metaphysical aspect as the Ground of Being). The experience of connection and oneness arises naturally because the essence of ourselves and the essence of everything else is the same essence. Something inside us (FrithjofSchuon termed it *intellectus*) intuits that this is so, even in our general state of ignorance, causing a restlessness that will not pass until we know the two as one. But what is the relationship between that experience and what is commonly called organized religion?

First, let's be clear there need not be any connection between the two. It's entirely possible that a person could have a full-blown experience of the "unitive knowledge" and no connection to religion whatsoever; conversely, many among the pious and faithful have never had a unitive mystical experience, nor do they consciously seek one. Many Perennialists prefer to go their own way and feel no need, nor see any benefit, in belonging to an organized religion. However, there are others who strongly disagree; for instance, as I've mentioned, the Traditionalists believe the traditional faiths are the most viable pathways, and a subset of them contends that those methods are the *only* pathways. Between these two extremes of "no religion" and "only religion" there is a range of viewpoints, though the ultimate prize for all Perennialists remains the experience of oneness with reality—which, after all, is not the goal of most organized religions, and traditional Judaism, for instance, doesn't include it at all.

A key perspective on the topic of religion within Perennialism was first drafted by the French mystic Rene Guenon (1886-1951) and later elaborated on by his student, the Swiss Sufi whom we've already mentioned several times, Frithjof Schuon (1902-1998). They argued that there are two distinct levels of religion. The first has the characteristics most readily associated with the word *religion*. When we say religion, it makes us think of one "ism" or another, including a specific dogma, a set of ceremonies, a moral code, a system of values, and a specific cultural tradition of art, architecture, and music. Guenon and Schuon refer to this level of religion as the *exoteric* or "outer" level, while, in addition, they posit an *esoteric* or "inner" level, dealing with mystical experiences. For Guenon, both these levels have value. For mystics, esoteric awakening may be the primary goal, but mystics have traditionally also been members of a society where exoteric religion generates a sense of communal identity and purpose. Furthermore, society itself has needs (as Sigmund Freud often pointed out), including the necessity of a shared code of behavior, as well as a shared cultural milieu to provide the context for living shared lives. Exoteric religion is beneficial in this regard, giving values and directives that generate social harmony. Moreover, exoteric religion sometimes contains the very structures and institutions that foster esoteric insight, including Buddhist *viharas*, Sufi *majlises*, Hindu *ashrams*, Jewish *yeshivas*, and the Greek Orthodox monasteries of Mt. Athos.

On the exoteric or outer level of religion, we find myriad differences between the faith traditions because these religions have grown up in unique parts of the world, with specific climates and during specific epochs of history, and these influences have had their effects, creating the distinctive cultures of the world. Consequently, these exoteric elements should not be quickly or impulsively abandoned according to Guenon and Schuon. But this is not the whole story of religion for Guenon, Schuon, or Huston Smith.

If we refocus our attention from the exoteric to the esoteric level, as we might refocus our eyes from the surface of a rushing stream to its quiet and motionless bottom, we find mystics from very different cultures saying very similar things about similar experiences. As F.C. Happold wrote in his landmark 1964 study of mysticism: "What, when one studies the mystical expressions of different religions, stands out most vividly, however, is not so much the differences as the basic similarities of vision." As we discussed earlier, the mystical traditions (rather than the organized religions themselves) can be thought of as different trails leading toward—in the case of the UME—a similar awakening; each trail with its own unique characteristics, like trails on an actual mountain, but these trails sometimes converge in the breakthrough experience of union with the Sacred—variously interpreted but with descriptive similarities as well as differences.

Touching back on the relationship of the perennial philosophy to organized religion, Huston Smith believed the "unitive knowledge" was the "core" of the world's mystical traditions, but not the core of organized or exoteric religion. Each religion, he believed, decides for itself what its core or essence is. He was simply offering a theory about mystical experiences related to which experience has the most value, and this is the viewpoint generally shared by Perennialists of the Traditionalist stripe.

In sharp contrast to Huston's view of organized religion, as we've seen, Huxley argued that religion is generally outdated and dangerous, and cultures need not be grounded in a religion to create shared identity or values. (Note that secularists, including environmentalists, may dislike religion but still have shared values and a collective identity.) Furthermore, Huxley felt that if religious leaders could recognize and admit that their religions, at best, are only means for reaching a goal, rather than goals in themselves, perhaps the faith traditions could be reformed in ways productive to the awakening of their believers. However, in the meantime, he thought they were blinded by dogmas that may comfort people who long for certainty but simultaneously bind them in views that distract them from waking up.

Huxley, Frederic Spiegelberg, Gerald Heard, and Alan Watts argued that organized religion is mainly the province of sycophants and obscurantists who dupe gullible sheep with various delusions, leaving mystical awakening, more often than not, discouraged, discarded or prevented. However, and as Huston Smith or Guenon would have asked Huxley or Spiegelberg, "Can't you entertain the thought that for the masses an experience of sitting in a beautiful cathedral listening to a choir sing J.S. Bach could give them a mystical experience?"

Summarizing briefly, and contrary to most opponents of the perennial philosophy, no Perennialist believes that the unitive mystical experience is the core of the organized religions. The Traditionalists believe it is the core of the mystical traditions exclusively, while "religion" operates on levels beyond the mystical, and each religion is free to judge what matters most to itself. In terms of Huxley's view, he believed the core of each religion is mainly a set of self-reinforcing delusions that should be abandoned. And while the unitive mystical experience is found in the mystical traditions, it too should not be thought of as a core or essence. As we've seen, he viewed it as an identifiable thread across the traditions, but didn't argue that every esoteric tradition gave it the same weight or value; some traditions, including certain forms of Hinduism and Sufism, place a premium on the unitive mystical experience, while others, including mainstream forms of Christianity and Judaism, give it less value than the experience of God's presence — favoring, as they do, an ontological separation between humans and their God. Consequently, in Huxley's Perennialism, the "unitive knowledge" or UME is the "highest common factor" of the mystical traditions but not their shared essential core—a core they all agree upon and therefore a variety of mystical essentialism or universalism.

Leaving off the various theories of how the perennial philosophy relates to both organized religion and the mystical traditions, if we side with the Huxley/Spiegelberg position and toss out organized religion entirely, where will people learn the pathways to awakening? And who will guide them? In the last fifty years, during what some historians of religion have dubbed the "Fourth Great Awakening," we've seen the emergence of a new approach to organized spirituality, one with a focus on self-development. Characteristics of this trend include attention placed on the sovereignty of personal choice ("I'll make up my own mind"); a dislike of dogmas ("No sacred cows for me, please!"); a willingness to explore new options ("I want to keep looking around"); a dislike of hierarchies ("I'd rather not prostrate myself before a sage-on-a-stage"); and an emphasis on direct experience ("I don't want to believe in something, I want to confirm it in my own life"). Furthermore, given these characteristics, we've witnessed the rise of institutions designed to accommodate them. The first of these was the Esalen Institute in Big Sur, California, founded in 1962 by Michael Murphy and Richard Price, but soon the Omega Institute in upstate New York followed, and today there are many others, large and small, including the 1440 Multiversity, the Kripalu Center for Yoga & Health, the Institute of Noetic Sciences, etc.

These highly inter-spiritual centers, where no particular perspective on human potentialities or how to develop them is set in stone, increasingly attract those who have either lost faith in organized religion or who wish to develop their spirituality beyond it. These centers have strong appeal for many Perennialists, especially those who increasingly identify as "spiritual but not religious," and it's no surprise that key Perennialists, including Huxley, Watts, Smith, Grof, Vaughan, and Ram Dass taught at such centers. This is the path that Chris Grosso and others have termed the "Indie" path of spiritual growth. "Indies" are seeking institutions where a plurality of methods is being tested (I personally call these places "Search Church"), including traditional methods but without any loyalty pledges. In addition to Indie spiritualists, these venues also attract those who practice what Wayne Teasdale called "inter-spirituality," which is why I used that term just a moment ago; it has become common parlance since Teasdale's death in 2004. This approach, which neither embraces organized religion nor speaks against it, borrows from all the traditional faiths to learn what works best for the individual. These inter spiritualists discern what's most valuable for themselves, jettisoning what they see as each religion's superfluous baggage. Inter-spiritualists say they can "take the best and leave the rest." But are they correct?

Schuon and Guenon, and today such Perennialists as Seyyed Hossein Nasr, James Cutsinger, and Harry Oldmeadow, dislike this cannibalizing approach to awakening, and especially if the conglomeration of views and practices borrowed from the mystical traditions includes elements from outside the religions. Their criticisms include that a "cafeteria approach" to spiritual life leads to behavior like that of a small child at a buffet: we take too much of what we want and too little of what we need. Furthermore, they argue, it's better to stay rooted in one's own tradition and dig a deep shaft of insight than wander around the landscape digging a series of shallow wells. The chance of striking spiritual water thus improves. However, in contrast to that view, Mirabai Starr, an avowed inter-spiritualist, retorts, "I'm not digging 'shallow wells.' I'm using various tools to dig a *very deep* well."

And who's to make the call? Organized religions provide some safety from charlatans and manipulators, but many philosophers (Sartre and Marx for instance) have argued that all religious functionaries are charlatans and manipulators. Furthermore, religious authorities can be guilty of dictating needs that are manufactured from within their own ideologies, scorning the views of other religions and obscuring the shared insights of their mystical traditions. And who's to say who's right?

The answer is not simple and the repercussions of any perspective take us beyond the boundaries of this short introduction to the perennial philosophy. In terms of Perennialism itself, the various viewpoints reveal again that it's a family of viewpoints rather than a homogenous outlook. My personal opinion, my advice, related to finding your own path, is to remember that methods only have value if they not only wake you up but make you a better person. If you decide to take the DIY "Indie" path, remember that you may be "throwing out the baby with the bathwater," given that religion can provide guidance and community. (Ramakrishna, the Hindu mystic, observed a century ago, "Religion is a cow that sometimes kicks but also gives milk.") Conversely, if you choose to accept an organized religion, keep open to the viability of other paths and hold onto the value of skepticism. As Paul Tillich, the Christian theologian, once remarked, "Doubt is not the opposite of faith, it is an aspect of faith."

GOD

"Knowledge of ourselves teaches us whence we came, where we are and whither we are going. We come from God and we are in exile; and it is because our potency of affection tends towards God that we are aware of this state of exile."

John van Ruysbroeck, thirteenth century

Christian mystic

"Silence is the language of God, all else is poor translation."

Jalal ud-Din Rumi

Up to this point we've touched on the notion of God only briefly, while describing the concept of the path of devotion. But what does the perennial philosophy say about the possible existence or importance of a Cosmic Designer, a Creator God, a Prime Mover, or Cosmic Mind who answers prayers and exists beyond space and time? Here too, predictably, we find a range of opinions. For instance, when discussing the God question, Ken Wilber gives a three-part answer, pointing out that the world's religions have generally conceived of "God" in three ways:

1. God as Self (the Great "I")
2. God as the Holy Other (the Great "Thou")
3. God as the Ground of Being (the Great "It")

The first of these we've already discussed in detail; it is the principle of the absolute aspect of our being. Furthermore, we've also investigated Wilber's third mode of God, the "Great It" which is the Ground of Being out of which all existence arises. And as we've seen also, that "Great It" is more of a God below than a God above, dealing, as it does, with what underlies existence rather than a divinity in the heavens. It is, in Plato's estimation, also the source of the clear light outside the Cave in his allegory, and it has as its purest qualities "Truth, Beauty, and Goodness." Consequently, when we awaken to "It," we are inspired to acknowledge and perpetuate these qualities in our lives.

But now we come to Wilber's second way of conceiving God, about which we've said very little. To begin, it's important to note that some Perennialists, including Huxley, agree with Buddhists that there is no Creator God who precedes creation and is responsible for it. In their view, creation lifts up into manifestation out of its own nature, operating on automatic pilot and with no need for a controller. Creation, they believe, occurs on a pulse, coming into existence and then (eons later) collapsing into quiescence, over and over again like the tide coming in and going out, with no original or *protogenic* event having ever taken place. For Buddhists, time is "beginningless" and exists only in a limited fashion during the periods of the coming-and-going cycles when the universe is in its manifesting phase. Some Perennialists agree with this view, while others—including today Rami Shapiro and Richard Rohr—do not, embracing a more Abrahamic position, including the notion of a *primogenitor* who set the universe in motion and continues to preside over it. Either way, what defines all Perennialists is their mutual embrace of the position Huxley related as the "minimum working hypothesis."

Moving along, one of the earliest proponents of the perennial philosophy was the German theologian Rudolf Otto, author of *The Idea of the Holy* (1917). Otto described God, the "Great Thou," as *ganz Andere* or "wholly Other" due to its uniqueness as an object of experience, and because it is unlike anything else, the experience of "It" can be both grand and frightening. Otto claimed the experience of this "numinous" Sacred is the root of all religions, an apprehension of a Mystery both "fascinating" and "tremendous," and not fully graspable by the rational mind. But this experience of God as the "Wholly Other" or Holy Other, a presence that can be evoked via devotion, can also, for most Periennialists, be joined with in ways that transcend the gap between It and us. On the level of daily experience, God is separate from our being, but on the level of the Ground of Being, on the level of what Meister Eckhart termed "Godhead," we merge into oneness.

Martin Lings and Seyyed Hossein Nasr are two Perennialists who embraced the Sacred as the "Great Thou," and both followed a traditional Sufi path to awakening. Sufis, the mystics of Islam, seek to wake themselves up by melting into the oneness of God, surrendering their will to that of Allah. Sufis describe human beings as *insan*, the "one who forgets"; consequently, they recite the ninety-nine names of Allah as a way of remembering Him—or more accurately, to *re-member—reconnect*—themselves to Him by joining their consciousness with His. This, all Sufis report, is an experience of pure joy and pure love, characterized as "divine drunken-ness," with the double meaning that an awakened Sufi may act intoxicated while having also been swallowed ("drunk") by God. They tell us God is Love and, contrary to the views of certain fanatics within Islam, they firmly argue that none of the ninety-nine names of Allah can be translated as the "Cruel," the "Hateful" or the "Vindictive."

In the fashion of these Sufis, other Great Thou Perennialists are generally monotheists. However, there are Hindu Perennialists (Arvind Sharma, Ananda Coomaraswamy, Rabindranath Tagore), who might seem to present a problem, given that Hindus worship many gods, right? Isn't that a contradiction of monotheism? Not really. Most Hindus believe that all gods are either *aspects of, creations of,* or *incarnations of* the One God, or I should say, the One God/Goddess entity. The *creations*—such as the spirits of nature—are not gods in the highest sense because they were created by God and have limitations like our own; even the grandest among them are only entities similar to the angels of the Abrahamic religions, far above us in terms of lifespan and majesty but not on a par with God. The *incarnations* of God are straightforward in that this simply means God sometimes takes form, for example as Krishna or Jesus Christ. The *aspects* of God are facets of the Great Thou's personality that loom to the forefront at different times, at least in human experience. They are like masks on the face of the One God, or like the spectrum of colors that emerge from the same white light. Sometimes God seems loving and sometimes He/She seems angry, and each of these "masks," male or female, can have a separate name according to its personality.

The majority of Perennialists who focus on the Great Thou view of God extends this Hindu conception (of one God underlying all the gods) to include gods beyond the Hindu pantheon, even if the focus of their personal practice is on one mask in particular. The psychologist Carl Jung, whom I and others consider a Perennialist, believed all gods are specific cultural manifestations of a "God Principle," a God *archetype* that arises in the human psyche because of our innate capacity to grasp the Sacred and personalize it.

Below the surface levels of our conscious mind, and even below our personal unconscious mind, we have a "transpersonal" strata of our psyche that Jung termed the "collective unconscious," and in this collective unconscious reside various archetypal symbols, personalities and narratives, including the God archetype. This archetype takes shape in *hierophanies* (various cultural forms) such as Christ, Zeus, Krishna, Gaia, Kuan Yin, Amaterasu, and Wakan Tanka but each is only a culture-specific embodiment of the same God principle. Several Perennialists, including Heinrich Zimmer, Mircea Eliade, and Joseph Campbell, were inspired by Jung's theory of archetypes and formulated complex systems of theology and mythology based on them. For more on the "one god who wears many masks" view of the Great Thou, I'd most recommend Campbell's series titled *The Masks of God*, and for more Perennialist views of the Great Thou, see also the works of Rudolf Otto, Raimon Panikkar, and Wayne Teasdale.

Beyond Ken Wilber's three ways of conceiving God, or perhaps existing as a sub-category of his second way, there are Perennialists today who follow the Terrance McKenna position that we must also consider the existence of a plurality of gods, nature spirits, or inter-dimensional entities. These beings, they say, are not projections of the mind but autonomous entities that have been recognized in myriad religions for eons. These include the *kami* of Shintoism, the fairy folk of the Celts, and the nature spirits of Native American religions, and working with them in our daily lives is useful to our physical and spiritual health. However, Perennialists who embrace the reality of these entities set their existence into the same context as that of all other living creatures, including ourselves. These are beings that may be grander or more insightful than us, but we share the same Ground of Being or World Soul with them, and experiencing that World Soul brings the "unitive knowledge" that remains the highest insight. Such beings may be very help-ful in solving daily problems, but they help best when they help us to fully awaken—that's the Perennialist position.

Given that you are now reading an introductory text, let's stop here in our analysis of the God topic, but to summarize, it may seem like there are atheistic Perennialists, who conceive of the Sacred only as the "Great I" or the "Great It," and theistic Perennialists who worship a personal God (the "Great Thou") or who seek to interact with a range of god-like spirits, and to some extent that summation is accurate. Huxley, Heard, Spiegelberg, and Watts doubted or denied the existence of a personal God, at best relegating it to the myth-generating tendencies of Jung's "collective unconscious." Furthermore, even among those who recognize and worship a personal God there is gener-ally an understanding that there is an amorphous Godhead at the wellspring of all existence, including God's existence. Consequently, even the personal relationship with God is ultimately transcended at the level where two, God and worshipper, become one.

At the other end of the pendulum swing, there are Perennialists who find fault entirely with the "Great It" idea, judging it as cold and impersonal, or who, like Buddhists, also find fault with the "Great I" viewpoint because it seems to suggest a permanent Self or ego. However, most Perennialists allow a range of perspectives, leaving it to the aspirant to decide which interpreta-tion best matches their experience.

10

ENLIGHTENMENT

"Enlightenment is only the wisdom of knowing you're everything and nothing at exactly the same time. Hence the power
and potency of paradox in myths, poetry and dreams."

Anonymous

"Be not simply good — be good for something."

Henry David Thoreau

In the world today, we generally recognize there are several states of human consciousness, and we place them within a rubric of "major" and "altered" states, based on both our subjective experiences of them and the physiological characteristics that attend them. The major states encompass waking, dreaming and sleeping, which are not only different from each other experientially but also because they have unique physical and neurological "signatures." For instance, rapid eye movement (REM) occurs only while we're dreaming, and delta rhythms, measured by an EEG, happen mainly during sleep. "Altered states of consciousness" are those that do not have significantly different physiological signatures from one or other of the major states but register slight differences in measurement and subjective experience. They are simply alterations of major states of consciousness, and so, for example, someone is drunk and awake or drunk and asleep but being drunk hasn't resulted in a state that is different enough to call it an additional "major state."

Among the major states, the west has historically placed a premium on the waking state of consciousness, believing it conveys the deepest apprehension of reality and is the most useful for the interests of daily life, while also recognizing the importance of sleeping and dreaming for general health (though there are differing theories about *why* dreaming is beneficial). However, if we broaden our investigation of conscious states to include testimony from all human cultures, we find a panoply of states of consciousness including meditative states, trance states, fugue states, hypnotic states, shamanic states, ecstatic states, states of possession, etc., and given this fact, where do these other states fit in?

In general, the west has ignored them or simply put them in the file of "useless experiences," with little or no interest in mapping their terrain. However, using other cartographic tools, traditional cultures have arrived at different conclusions, creating their own schemes about which states are most valuable for assessing (and accessing) Reality with a capital R. Are these other cultures wrong? If we think of states of consciousness as analogous to channels on a television set, are there only a few channels on the human "TV" or is it that we have only been watching a few and wrongly thinking they're all that's available?

From the Perennialists' perspective, and that of mystics in general, the latter is the case. We have relied too heavily on the waking state, and even then, only on a limited, robotic, blinkered interpretation of it. In our ignorance, we are like a color-blind person who mistakes their monochromatic experience for the only possibility of human vision. With regards to altered and expanded states of consciousness, we are, as others have colorfully put it, "third eye blind."

Describing all the various states of consciousness termed "mystical" is beyond the scope of this small book, though a very interesting topic. Our purpose here is to outline the Perennialist perspectives on one particular state: the UME.

Perennialists place an emphasis on this particular mystical state, and it's significant to note that a majority of mystics have also. In her landmark book *Mysticism* (1911), Evelyn Underhill, a Christian, pointed this out after analyzing the many states described in the mystical literature. "Mysticism," she offered as a general definition, "is the art of union with Reality. The mystic is a person who has attained that union." When the individual realizes experientially that the root of their being is synonymous with the root of all being, consciousness reaches—at least briefly—a cosmic proportion. This instigates a wholesale revolution in one's consciousness, leading Perennialists to label the awakening not only an additional major state of consciousness but the most valuable state.

Maurice Bucke labeled this highest state of consciousness "Cosmic Consciousness" (the title of his 1901 bestseller), and the traditional mystics, as we've seen, have given it other names as well, including *fana, jivanmukta, bodhi,* and *gnosis.* For Teresa of Avila, it was the "highest stage of contemplation." It was also the highest goal of what biologist Loren Eiseley called the "Immense Journey," and he and other Perennialists are in agreement on that point, since this state of consciousness fulfills the last two axioms of Huxley's "minimum working hypothesis" (see chapter 3). However, they disagree over some of the features and details of this highest state, and these differences are important to consider if we wish to understand the range of Perennialist viewpoints.

First of all, is the unitive experience *permanent* or *episodic*? In other words, does awakening based on an *ontic* expansion of the individual (or, more accurately, an expansion of the individual's cognizance of their actual ontology) persist as a continuing feature of their everyday experience, resulting in a greatly enhanced waking state of consciousness, or does it come and go in temporary bursts of rapture? Here, as with other topics we've discussed, we find several opinions, but these are not segregated into the same divisions we've seen between Traditionalists and the liberal Perennialists such as Huxley and Watts. Guenon, and Schuon (both Traditionalists), but also Huxley and Watts, agreed that a continuous state of consciousness at full aperture (analogous to the *nirvana* state claimed by Buddhists) is possible. It may begin with transitory flashes of awakening in advance of the final breakthrough but continuous "enlightenment" is possible. In contrast, Huston Smith and others have argued that our "mortal coils" are too strong for us to break entirely free, and consequently even mystics keep falling from rapture, resettling into a more limited and less cosmically integrated state of consciousness. This return, they argue, is due to our conditioned responses to the world, our confined tendencies of perception, and the draws of daily life.

Saying all this, wouldn't the awakened state have to be continuous if we were to call it "enlightenment?" This depends on how we define *enlightenment*. For Huston Smith, even brief awakenings to what we truly are can provide the necessary adjustment to our perspective, as even a small reprieve from Plato's Cave would cause a revolution in the thoughts of the prisoners who broke free. Imagine also that a person who had been blind since birth somehow, even if only for a few hours, could see the world as you and I do right now. Would that experience cause a reformation in their understanding of the world? How could it not! To change someone's perception of reality even briefly is to change reality itself for them permanently.

Going a step further, there are those like Colin Wilson who have argued that falling back into our everyday consciousness is actually necessary and beneficial, because alternating our consciousness between the cosmic perspective and our default-waking-state mode generates a kind of binocular vision that is more than the sum of its parts. By returning to Plato's Cave, even if it requires a loss of the light outside, we gain insight into the light's value; moreover, we are better able to gauge the plight of other 'prisoners' and sympathize with them. In brief, Wilson believed the loss of cosmic consciousness is a sacrifice valuable to the process of spiritual maturation. Put another way, he believed that losing continuous enlightenment is essential for insuring another, and higher, state of enlightenment.

Disagreements between Perennialists even exist among those who believe cosmic consciousness can be held permanently. Some describe the condition as do Hindus and Buddhists, seeing it as a state of on-going perfection in which one has access to all knowledge (of all sorts) and can do no wrong morally, while others theorize that perfection, even for the person in cosmic consciousness, is both impossible and undesirable. These believe the ideal of the "perfect person" exists only as an archetype, in the way that the goddess Venus embodies the archetype of the perfectly beautiful woman or Hercules embodies the archetype of the perfectly strong man. For those in this latter camp, the archetype of the perfect person (say Christ or the Buddha) is valuable as an ideal to aspire towards but does not and cannot exist in the flesh. It is an ideal and an ideal only.

Those in this camp (which also has its sub-schools) generally believe that even if one experienced an on-going state of cosmic consciousness they would still be influenced by the limitations of their mortal coils, i.e., their body-minds. They would retain relative influences on their minds inherited from having been born in a certain place, at a certain time, to a certain family, and with a particular set of values, habits and customs. These influences form a psychological context through which the unitive knowledge is then filtered. A breakthrough, whether temporary or permanent, may have occurred but that experience is then interpreted and expressed by a body-mind that speaks a particular language, has a certain level of intelligence, and has been privy to a limited palette of concepts. Summarizing this particular position, awakening may be on-going and yet perfection still doesn't occur.

These Perennialists warn that danger occurs if the person having the continuous experience jumps to the conclusion that they are now finished or perfect. For instance, if the self-aggrandizing aspect of the ego remains alive, even as only an unconscious sliver of its former self, it can attach to the unitive experience, claiming ownership of it, even to the point of moving from thinking "I am one with God" to claiming "I am God." The history of the so-called "consciousness movement" for the past fifty years has provided numerous examples of gurus and "enlightened masters" who have made this mistake. I'm reminded of a story Huston Smith told me to illustrate this point.

Huston and I were chatting about experiences we had had in India and the "mystic east." He asked if I had ever witnessed a miracle and I answered unequivocally, no. But then I amended my answer, adding, "Well, maybe." I told Huston about a time when I had witnessed a Hindu swami who willed himself to die. The man was very old and suffering from several maladies, so he decided to "let go of his body," making plans for when he would die and asking his devotees to attend the event. I was not a devotee but he invited me to come, and out of respect, I sat, two days later, with his group in silence while he meditated on a stage in front of us. Then, a few hours later, he died peacefully while maintaining a seated posture.

Huston was engrossed by my story, but then offered that he could do me one better. He had witnessed something similar, except that the swami in his case had begun and ended his vigil while positioned in a headstand. "No easy task!" Huston pointed out. Huston had been astounded by what he saw, so when he returned to the house where he was staying with Indian friends, he couldn't contain his excitement. After telling his hosts about what had happened, he expected them to be equally amazed, but the man of the house was actually nonplussed, shrugging the whole thing off as no big deal. "Well, he always was a show-off!" the man observed. This raises the question: can ego persist even in an awakened yogi? Huston believed it could.

Most Perennialists, whether they believe awakening can be permanent or only episodic (or, like Colin Wilson, permanent *because* it's episodic) agree that there is always room for spiritual growth, even in the awakened state. Each day there are new opportunities to nourish ourselves and discover what we are as embodied beings. And even if cosmic consciousness and the UME can be experienced continuously, what about the various aspects of the body-mind that could still be developed? For instance, what about emotional growth? Huston Smith would want to ask the person who claims perfection, "OK, so you're continuously experiencing the unitive knowledge, but how do you get along with your mother? Can she still push your buttons during holiday gatherings? If so, you've still got work to do," and related to this point, Jack Kornfield once observed, "Even the best meditators have old wounds to heal." Similarly, Ken Wilber has argued that reaching spiritual maturity does not only require us to "wake up" but also to "clean up," by facing our emotional baggage, and "grow up," in terms of taking responsibility for our actions.

Phil Novak, who was a graduate student of Huston Smith's at Syracuse University, has a theory of awakened consciousness that I find very interesting. Phil once told me, during a conversation in his office at Dominican University, that "Enlightenment may be an *asymptote*." When I made a quizzical face, he explained that in mathematics the principle of an asymptote is commonly illustrated with a graph that has both a vertical and a horizontal axis, forming a backwards "L" (visually like the bottom right corner of this page or the cover of this book). The horizontal axis represents the lapse of time and the vertical axis represents the growth of consciousness from ignorance to enlightenment. Over time, and starting at the left of the graph, near the bottom of the backwards "L," we find the point that represents the start of growth toward self-actualization. At first, the line starts running parallel to the horizontal axis (the axis of time), on course to eventually touch the vertical axis on the right; however, as time elapses the line of self-actualization begins to climb, forming the trajectory of our growth toward awakening—but, paradoxically, also keeping the line of our development from quickly reaching the vertical axis. Our spiritual growth keeps getting closer to the axis of perfection but as our enlightenment quotient rises (and perhaps *because* our enlightenment quotient rises) we never reach or touch it. Novak told me he believes this is the asymptotic nature of our growth, and I've generally embraced his idea as my own Huxleyan "working hypothesis." There will always be room for growth, which, frankly, I interpret as a wonderful thing. Who would want all their growth to stop? Trying to achieve such a state of completion is, according to a friend of mine, "like trying to eat once and for all." But as we've seen, other Perennialists disagree.

11

SCIENCE AND KNOWING

"It would be possible to describe everything scientifically, but it would make no sense; it would be without meaning, as if you described a Beethoven symphony as a variation of wave pressure."

Albert Einstein

*B*ertrand Russell, the British analytical philosopher, once wrote, "What science cannot prove, mankind cannot know," but what if he was mistaken? What if there are areas of knowledge, and even ways of knowing, that escape the scientific method but are nonetheless effective and valuable to our lives? What if we as a culture are drawing wrong conclusions about reality from science's current inability to fully grasp what reality *is* (at least in terms of the human relationship to it), in the way that a fisherman might wrongly suppose there is no ocean around his boat because none of it has come up in his net? In other words, could we be mistaking science's inability to catch life's deeper meaning for proof that none exists, confusing, as Huston Smith once put it, "an absence of evidence for evidence of absence?"

Perennialists generally believe this is the case; meaning and purpose—at least at the highest level of insight—have escaped the methods of science because science has the wrong set of tools for apprehending them, and we, as a society, have refused to explore methods beyond science, in the way that medieval Christians once couldn't conceive of—or allow—science as an alternative way of knowing to religion. Perennialists accept without question that science is deeply valuable, and its methods are legitimate ways of knowing many things, but its summations shouldn't be confused for the whole story of what and how it is possible to know. "And why not?" you may ask.

Science is effective when dealing with weights and measures, but there are whole areas of human concern (arguably, the primary ones) where science gets no traction at all—that is, areas where it can't *know*. Collectively, these areas of concern involve our subjective interaction with the world and are termed "issues of *qualia*," since they deal with *qualitative* assessments, rather than *quantitative* ones. In philosophy, the term *qualia* technically refers to the felt or phenomenal qualities of our subjective interface with the world; it deals with what it's like to know pain or hear sound or see color. For instance, the color blue is a subjective, qualitative experience of a particular wavelength of light (note that the wavelength can be quantified but the blue itself only exists in our experience) and to know the experience of blue is to know its *qualia*. I'm bringing this up because the term can be—and sometimes is—expanded to include the entire domain of qualitative experiences, such as those related to moral values, ethical concerns, experiences of love and beauty, tastes in music, art and food, and—as we will see—spiritual experience. For instance, science can quantify how many paintings are on display in an art museum (simply by counting them), but it has no ability to tell us which of them is *best*. It can quantify the number of paintings but not their *quality*. In fact, science cannot even prove that art is in the museum, given that "art" is a subjective assessment (which is why some people see art where others do not). In short, we may know what art is, but science does not. We may know what "music" is, but science finds only vibration.

To give but one more example of the limitations of science related to qualia, science can prove that eating too many fatty foods will reduce our chances for a long life, but it can't tell us we shouldn't choose a shorter life filled with donuts, cakes and French fries over a longer life without them. The choice of which is *better* (a *qualia* word) will depend upon our subjective metrics for gauging a good life. Science can offer facts we should consider when making life choices, including that fatty foods aren't healthy, but it can't make the final call. As Philip Goff, a contemporary philosopher of consciousness studies, puts it in *Galileo's Error*, "The data of observation and experiments can tell us how best to achieve our goals. But it's hard to see how an experiment or an observation could tell us what goals we ought to adopt in the first place." In fact, given that so much of our lives deal with the domain of *qualia* (the domain of our subjective responses to the world) Leo Tolstoy once sadly remarked, "Science is meaningless because it gives us no answer to our question, the only question important for us: what shall we do and how shall we live?"

What makes for a good life? Is it wrong to cheat and lie? Is Shakespeare a better author than Chaucer? Should I care about my neighbors? Does my wife love me? Does sushi taste delicious or yucky? Is it beneficial that I get out of bed tomorrow morning? Was the Buddha a wise person? Is the "Mona Lisa" a beautiful painting? Is rap music crap or is it "dope?" These are *qualia* questions. And it's an odd fact of our world today that materialist philosophers reject out of hand the possibility that reality has a metaphysical aspect (a dimension beyond the physical), such as a Ground of Being. For if we shift our discussion of reality from ontological possibilities to epistemic concerns (those that deal with knowing), materialists rarely note that metaphysics is alive and well. We claim to *know* things every day that are beyond physics (that is, unprovable by science), including that our parents love us, that music is beautiful, and that racial discrimination is immoral.

This is deeply important to acknowledge. First, because it makes clear that what sometimes is called "value-free science" doesn't actually exist; in fact, it's one of the great philosophical delusions of our time. This is not to say that scientific facts aren't real. They are. For instance, the atomic weight of boron will always be 10.81 and water will always be composed of oxygen and hydrogen. But the facts of science have no value until they are applied to the circumstances of life, and *whenever we apply them, a qualia related decision has been made.* Note again that even if we have science-based reasons for why we should make them, we have still made choices science can't prove definitively right or wrong.

In fact, science's inability to confirm what the good life should be, or whether or not there is such a thing as a good life, has cast us into a morass of absolute relativism. Today, more and more people, not understanding science's blind spot, argue that if you can't quantify a *qualia* choice, then any other choice is just as good. For instance, if you can't prove why Chopin's music is preferable to street noise, then saying so is little more than stating a personal preference. And this relativizing tendency, catalyzed by the illusion that only what science can quantify as true is true, has an even more pernicious effect when we consider moral values. Is it immoral to lie and cheat? "Who says so?" a teenager might ask, "How can you *prove* it?" In fact, this mistaken understanding—that if you can't prove a *qualia* decision scientifically it isn't more valid than any other—explains why so many young people today feel lost in a world of absolutely relative choices, and why we find so much rampant cynicism—for instance, based on the view that a life of selfishness and slothful behavior is just as *good* as any other sort of life. In summary, an embrace of science alone will never free civilization from the possibility of barbarism (as the Nazis have already proven). Only expansions of the heart and mind will do that, and *that* is what inner knowing is all about.

Perennialists maintain that inner knowing is another epistemic tool, another means of gaining valid and meaningful knowledge. Consequently, Perennialists are part of what Nicholas Langlitz, an anthropologist working today, has termed the "epistemic counter-culture." They don't wish to drop science, they wish to add noetic insight to the toolbox. The UME has a different character than the concept-based knowledge of science, so it is not something that we know like the atomic weight of boron, but it has profound implications for our daily choices in life. Perennialists contend that expanding the size of our inner space informs our perspective on what is *best* for us by expanding our insight into who we are, forming a wider, more wholistic platform for qualia decisions. For instance, if I experience myself as interrelated with all of life, I will care more about others because I will more deeply identify with them.

Of course, materialists will argue that Perennialists are making this assumption based on an unproven theory that we have an aspect of our being that transcends our individuality, but it's important to note that materialists are already making qualia decisions based on their own unproven theory that we do not. Furthermore, there is every reason today to believe that these two ways of knowing, scientific (outer) and noetic (inner), can work together to help us arrive at the most qualitatively desirable world possible. Rupert Sheldrake has pointed out in *Ways to Go Beyond and Why They Work* (2019) that the Greek word for experience, *emperiria,* is the root of our English word empirical, and "the exploration of consciousness through consciousness itself is literally empirical, based on experience." We can confirm or contend against the noetic claims of others via our own inner experiences. Is it possible to experience the unitive mystical experience? Scientists can find out for themselves by running experiments with their own minds, and nobody is asking them to believe it out-of-hand.

"The self-imposed separation between science and the spiritual realm is breaking down," Sheldrake believes, "as scientists investigate spiritual practices and as the field of consciousness studies develops.... Systematic research into experiences brought about by spiritual practices brings science and spirituality into convergence. This new synergy could lead towards better ways of relating to the realm of more-than-human consciousness, and also to deepening our understanding of spiritual experiences."

Inner awakening brings insight, imagination and vision to guide our *qualia* decisions toward our own life and the world around us, and science can help us confirm or deny that we're getting where we want to go, even as it looks more deeply into the neurologic nature and therapeutic value of having UMEs. Science will always have its place, helping to inform our qualia decisions without making them for us. Meanwhile, Perennialists believe we should open our minds to the possibility that exploring inner space has at least as much value as exploring outer space.

What might our future as a species be if we come to know ourselves experientially as deeply entwined with all existence? Perennialists of all stripes are hoping we find out.

12

LOVE

"Am I a man, a woman, an angel, or even a pure soul? I do not know for Love has melted these words away. Now I am free of all these images that haunted my busy mind."

Hafez

"Love is the astrolabe of God's secrets. This way or that, love guides all to eternity. Words may enable us to understand, but ineffable love…is the best enlightener."

Jalal ud-Din Rumi

Love is a strong emotion that has been described and defined in myriad ways, including that it's a feeling of extreme appreciation for another person. However, starting at the top, so to speak, love is also commonly referred to as a universal force beyond emotion—more like the 1960s counterculture's view of LOVE as the soul of nature and what's conveyed in the expression "God is Love." In this regard, it's the heart-felt and *soul-felt* equivalent of what happens when one opens their consciousness to the Ground of Being, exclaiming as did Huxley, that "Everything is All Right. Capital A. Capital R." One becomes flooded with the feeling of being embraced by the Sacred (capitalized here to suggest its absolute nature), and can't help but recognize that the Sacred's very nature, interpreted through the heart and soul, feels like pure Love.

And what if we could, on a personal level, hold onto this feeling and cognition that we are deeply loved or perhaps actually floating inside Love itself? The Romantic poets, as well as the hippies of the 1960s, espoused that conviction, and though the cynic within us may scoff at such sentiment, most mystics have shared it. Mirabai, Rumi, St. John of the Cross, and more recently Kahil Gibran and the guru Ammachi, come readily to mind in this regard.

Maharishi Mahesh Yogi, remembered as The Beatles' guru, often remarked that when one is awakened to the true nature of things, one constantly feels cradled in the world. Like the child who at times, when playing by themselves, feels a moment of loneliness or fear only to then remember that they are safe because "Mother is at home," the mystic, submerged in the pure *gnosis* of awakening, feels at home wherever they find themselves. They belong to the world and reside in its cosmic embrace. Even when relative circumstances are not blissful, Love provides a perspective on life's challenges that inspires gratitude, as with the Christian martyr who, after being dragged behind a Roman chariot, mumbled as his last words, "Gratitude. Gratitude for everything."

This is not to say that if one experiences universal love they don't care about daily concerns or feel any need to engage in practical matters, believing everything is already perfect. The dishes still must be washed and the house should still be cleaned. Practical matters will continue to matter. Making the same point, when George Harrison was once asked, twenty years after the release of the "Sgt. Pepper's" album, if he still believed, "All You Need is Love," he answered, "Yeah, I'll stick with that—but I'll add something else: 'All you need is love—and a sandwich.'" Daily concerns, and even unpleasant challenges, will remain, but, nonetheless, Love triumphs over all and informs every circumstance.

Sometimes the cosmic embrace feels so deeply personal that a natural desire to reciprocate springs up. In this way, some Perennialists are drawn to the path of devotion to God or the Goddess, sensing, as they do, that the Ground of Being is not only pure sentience but also sentient in a very human way; that is, awake like we are but on a much grander scale. Many of these aspirants are drawn by Love to renounce all else, the better to focus on this Divine Presence, loving it with all their heart and soul. Expressions of their love then flow from them as music, art, poetry, and architecture; for instance, we witness such devotional love in Rabindranath Tagore's poem, "I Want

Thee, Only Thee," from his book *Gitanjali*, for which he won the Nobel Prize in 1913:

> That I want thee, only thee—let my heart
> repeat without end. All desires that distract me,
> day and night, are false and empty to the core.
>   As the night keeps hidden in its gloom the petition
>   for light, even thus in the depth of my unconsciousness
> rings the cry—I want thee, only thee.
> As the storm still seeks its end in peace
> when it strikes against peace with all its might,
> even thus my rebellion strikes against thy love
> and still its cry is—I want thee, only thee.

Other Perennialists, depending upon what Huston Smith terms their "spiritual personality type" (since that's what determines their inclinations), may decide to serve God by serving others, extending the Sacred's love for creation by taking care of its creatures and the natural world in which they live. (Today I'd place Andrew Harvey, Mirabai Starr, Rami Shapiro, and Richard Rohr in this category.) And even those atheistic or impersonalist Perennialists—like Huxley or Gerald Heard—who interpret the Sacred's quality of omniscience to mean only that consciousness is everywhere (because the universe is made of consciousness), rather than aware of everything, may be drawn toward service. The Godhead or Oversoul is everywhere for them but they do not interpret that to mean the Sacred is consciously aware of each discrete moment of time and space. Instead, they lend their hands and hearts to service so that universal Love may not only exist but be felt in the world. For Perennialists, the perspective that God is Love is not only a personal comfort but an impetus to love the world back by helping those with whom we share it. Love might express itself in a beautiful piece of art, a song or painting in tribute and celebration of the world, or it may manifest as loving kindness toward needful strangers. The point being that Love is open, expressive, supportive of the will, and never selfish.

And where, if at all, does romantic love between two people fit into this scheme of things? Many mystics have been monks and ascetics who renounced the world, including the physical and emotional pleasures of romantic love; for instance, the Tibetan mystic Milarepa lived in a cave and starved himself, eating only nettles to instigate his final breakthrough. Similarly, the Desert Fathers of early Christianity wandered in the Sinai, and the Hindu saint Tulsidas reached enlightenment only after leaving his wife and family. And in agreement with this approach, a few Perennialists, including Gerald Heard, have argued that romantic love inspires so much attachment and craving that it becomes difficult, if not impossible, to free one's mind of their influences and attachments. Like Theravada Buddhists, they believe the surest and fastest path to awakening is a solitary one. Better to express Love through humanitarian service than the entanglements of affection. Romantic love may be possible once we're free of our ignorant tendencies and in control of ourselves but not before.

However, the majority of Perennialists disagree with this "leave the world behind" perspective, accepting a position common in Tantric philosophy that we can be bound in ignorance as surely by our aversions as by our desires, given that unhealthy attachments can adhere to both sides of the equation. For instance, if a man were to join the Catholic priesthood or a Buddhist monastery out of fear of becoming attached to their lustful thoughts or domestic affections, he might grow to hate the women or men to whom he's attracted because they inspire desire. Attachment to this hatred, and the aversion it's likely to generate, might deepen if the lust can neither be released nor overcome. Furthermore, the desire for intimacy and nurturing arises naturally in the human heart (as Judaism has long contended), so one might become emotionally stunted, bitter and neurotic if these feelings are constantly denied and demonized. Apropos of this, there is a story in the literature of Chinese Buddhism illustrating the point—and by now you've realized I like a good story.

While walking along a country road on their way to a monastery where they will spend the night, two monks—one young and one old—come upon a beautiful young woman who is stymied in her ability to cross a stream. She is wearing an exquisite silk dress and is afraid the water will ruin it. To help her on her way, the old monk wades into the stream and bends over in front of the young woman, saying "Get on my back and I will carry you across," which she promptly does. This shocks the young monk, since Buddhist monks vow never to touch a woman or let a woman touch them. So he crosses the stream in silence, completely embarrassed, and, after the woman thanks the old monk, the two men continue on their way.

Hours go by and then, during their last rest period before reaching their lodgings for the night, the old monk says, "Usually you are talkative while we are traveling, but this afternoon you have been quiet. Why is that?" To which the young monk, who is red in the face, blurts out, "Master, we have taken a vow never to touch a woman but today you have not only let a woman climb on your back, you have held her thighs as you carried her across the stream. This is forbidden!" The old monk sighs, looks into the eyes of the young monk and replies, "I set that woman down five hours ago. When will you put her down?" The old monk carried her for ten minutes, while the young monk dwelled upon her for many hours.

The moral of the story is that attachment to the letter of the law (not to mention an aversion to women) had blinded the young monk to the law's intent; the goal of renunciation is to overcome attachment in all forms, not only to our desires but also to their direct opposite, our aversions. Even if there may be wisdom in living alone (at least for a while, and especially if efforts toward awakening are constantly set aside for the sake of cheap thrills), romantic love, including torrid sexuality, can not only be healthy but the path to awakening.

Perennialists taking this latter position believe we can find our way to the Ground of Being and the unitive knowledge through the beloved, for the Ground, Oversoul, or Godhead is the foundation of the beloved's being as well as our own. In fact, the magic and beauty we see in the beloved is not just the product of their unique personality but of their unique way of express-ing the Ground of Being. When we look into their eyes and see the deepest recesses of who they are (i.e., when, as we say, we "see their soul"), we also find the deepest recess of the Oversoul; that is, we discover who *we* most are by finding out who *they* most are.

In romantic love, we discover one of several contexts in which univer-sal Love can move back and forth between two poles. To mix metaphors, a dynamic of reflected and reflexive appreciation is created analogous to two mirrors facing each other to form an infinite regress. We "love" the beloved, but who they most deeply *are* is the Oversoul, the Ground of Being, so over time we—who are also that Ground—perceive them less as "my beautiful wife, Stephani," and more as the Oversoul expressing, enjoying and celebrating itself as Stephani. We find our way to universal Love through a particular love, and eventually we live in a condition where infinite Love is celebrating itself in a particular dualistic context.

Whatever the object of love, whether a lover, a child, God, a pet, humanity or the planet earth, if that love is free of selfishness, it will lead toward universal Love. And once there, we undergo a reorientation of the heart akin to the reorientation of the mind that also follows awakening. We realize that our love did not come from us (as a particular body-mind) but rather *through us* from LOVE itself. Gibran once alluded to this dynamic beautifully when he wrote, "When you love, you should not say 'God is in my heart', but rather, 'I am in the heart of God.'"

As a last word here: what about the person who perhaps experiences the Ground of Being otherwise? That is, what about the person who has an UME and finds the experience scary or disorienting rather than blissful or as an undifferentiated field of LOVE? Such scary experiences are found in the traditional literature, as well as in the accounts of present day psychedelic psychonauts. From a Perennialist perspective, these experiences most commonly arise when an individual's ego feels challenged by the experiential realization that it can be set aside, transcended, or thrust into internal spaces where it has no control or holds no domain. This "ego death," as it's often called, can feel terrifying and hardly desirable. In fact, in Tibetan Buddhism, it's claimed that even Buddhas such as Amitabha and Manjushri appear fierce and terrifying to those who clutch onto their *ahamkar* or "ego" (hence the "demonic" forms of the Buddhas in Tibetan art), as the police may also seem like the "bad guys" to be avoided in the minds of actual criminals. But with the right attitude (including a willingness to allow that the ego is only one voice inside one's psyche), Perennialists believe a transmutation can take place in which the psychonaut realizes what seemed threatening was only a Love too gigantic for the ego—at least at first—to comprehend.

13

PSYCHOLOGY

"For Jung, the unconscious was a populous mythological pantheon. Freud saw it rather as an underground urinal, scribbled over…with four-letter words."

Aldous Huxley

"I think that much of our depression, anxiety, and addiction has to do with what John [of the Cross] writes about: the soul's need and longing for transcendence. This need is instinctual and unavoidable."

Mirabai Starr

What is the nature of the human psyche? What are its constituent parts? To what extent are our daily thoughts and actions influenced by our subconscious minds? What constitutes sanity and insanity? To what extent can an insane person become sane?

These questions and others were the early focus of psychology, before it turned toward behaviorism, and though they continue to have relevance for the field, the medical establishment has reached no consensus on any of these matters. Several models of the psyche currently exist, and the list of its primary motivations is far from being settled. However, related to Perennialism, we find that some schools of psychology are more compatible with its general viewpoint than others; for instance, "humanistic psychology" is commonly cited, including the works of Frances Vaughan, Stanislav Grof, and Abraham Maslow.

For instance, Maslow, like Huxley, argued that we have latent human potentialities that are our world's most important undeveloped natural resources; consequently, he believed the best psychology would not only help neurotic and psychotic people become sane but help sane people become *more sane*, reaching new and higher levels of clarity, insight, and emotional stability. Like William James, Frederic Myers, C.G. Jung and only a few other psychologists before him, Maslow was more interested in the higher end of the psyche's functionality than its dysfunctional pathologies, and in this regard, he considered that human beings were likely to have metaphysical and "transpersonal" aspects of their psyches reaching far beyond what many considered the limits of the "mind."

In *Motivation and Personality* (1954), Maslow first laid out what he termed the psyche's "hierarchy of needs," a perspective he developed further in his book *Toward a Psychology of Being* (1962). Where Sigmund Freud had explained we have a primal set of drives, Maslow determined that Freud's list was far too short and much too primal. Yes, we have drives for food, shelter, sleep and sex, but that is not the whole story. Maslow believed the full list of our drives can be arranged into a hierarchy (often depicted as a pyramid) with Freud's primal drives forming only the first tier of the structure, and with our higher motivations stacked on top of it in stages, reaching toward a summit of psychological fulfillment he termed "self-actualization."

After our most basic needs are met, new and increasingly sophisticated drives awaken in minds as other aspects of our psyche demand to be heard. Moving up the pyramid away from only the drives for food, shelter and sex, we find that we also have (1) a drive for safety and security that leads us to join communities; (2) a desire to love and be loved that causes us to form relationships and start families; (3) a drive for self-esteem and meaningful work; and finally, at the pinnacle of our development, (4) a drive to know who we are in the fullest sense. The lower stages, inclusive of our most basic drives, Maslow referred to as "deficiency needs" because they deal with things that we lack (such as food and shelter); however, the higher stages of our growth deal with "meta-needs" that flow from the drive to self-actualize and creatively express ourselves. Maslow believed everyone has these higher needs, however latent or undeveloped they may be, but he speculated that only about .005 percent of the population is concerned with achieving them.

This is why the foundation of the pyramid is so much larger than its pinnacle, and why, quite frankly, so many people find artists and spiritual seekers delusional and impractical, though in reality they are anything but. Artists and seekers, Maslow contended, sense more clearly the value of self-actualization, however vague that drive may seem to the majority.

To illustrate the highest level of development, Maslow compiled a list of people he believed had achieved it, including not only Thomas Jefferson and Eleanor Roosevelt but also Aldous Huxley, William James, Ralph Waldo Emerson, Walt Whitman, John Muir, and several others whose views resonate, I believe, with the perennial philosophy. Investigating the biographies of these people, Maslow determined that in almost all cases they had reported their highest insights resulted from what Maslow termed "peak experiences." These breakthrough moments in their lives were characterized by a mystical sense of timelessness, transcendence and ecstasy, as well as strong feelings of love and connectedness with all reality, and Maslow saw in these experiences realms of psychological inquiry that had long been ignored, mainly due to an entrenched materialism in the field of psychology.

What if our psyches *do* have metaphysical aspects that reach beyond our physical bodies? And what if connecting with these aspects can lead to self-actualization? And what if staying cut off from these aspects of what we are is at least one cause of mental illness and emotional instability? What if the Divine Ground of Being actually exists? And what if the experience of it can trigger the fullest blossoming of the psyche? Maslow thought these questions were at least worth considering, even if they were generally taboo in his academic circles.

Maslow speculated that we often suffer and mope around at the bottom of the hierarchy of needs because of our culture's entrenched fixation on them, which has wrongly convinced us that if we're not yet happy, we only need to acquire more of what we already have. We need more food, bigger houses and sexier partners, rather than chasing after delusional spiritual experiences or attending self-help seminars. Fulfillment is possible, but only if we seek it within the framework of our everyday, so-called practical desires. Maslow disagreed. For him, fulfillment of the richest sort will only come when we grasp the transcendental roots of our nature, and each time we catch a glimpse of THAT, a peak experience occurs.

Furthermore, Maslow contended that by accumulating more and more of these peak experiences, through whatever means possible, whether by attending symphonies, sitting in meditation, or taking a psychedelic substance, we move toward self-actualization. He referred to this method of evolving "Being-cognition therapy" because, having heard the testimonies of those who had achieved the summit of the hierarchy of needs, he felt their awakening had depended upon experiences of a transcendent level of self or being. This, of course, sounds familiar because you've read about it in Part II of this book. Maslow's work gave rise to a whole branch of psychology termed "Transpersonal Psychology," so named because it allows consideration of levels of the psyche that stretch all the way to Oversoul.

Building off of Maslow's work, a cadre of transpersonal psychologists arose during the 1970s, including Frances Vaughan, Richard Tarnas, Ira Progoff, Anthony Sutich, and Stanislav Grof. Moreover, transpersonalism is alive today at the Esalen Institute, and at The Institute of Noetic Sciences, Naropa University, Sofia University, the California Institute of Integral Studies and elsewhere. Ken Wilber continues to be a primary theorist of transpersonal views, and these views resonate deeply with perennialism. For instance, in *No Boundary* (1979), Wilber describes the self-actualized state as one of "Supreme Identity" with all reality, an iteration of what Huxley called the "unitive knowledge," and in Wilber's scheme, the psyche is, ideally, liberating itself from various degrees of delusional separation. These separations are delusional because they are based on partial consideration of all that we are.

The ego, in its unactualized state, feels itself separate from various other aspects of the mind-body and exterior world, but these separations are mutable and can be transcended. For instance, the ego can learn to grow beyond its disdain for certain aspects of its host psyche that it doesn't like. Integrating these disliked, disowned and repressed aspects of who we are (Jung termed these aspects our "Shadow"), creates a widening of who we are in the direction of "no boundaries"—and the expansion does not end there.

Eventually, consciousness reaches the point where we awaken to the fact that what we truly are transcends all boundaries, causing an integration with reality at a cosmic scale, which is Wilber's, as well as Maslow's, definition of total sanity. To achieve this self-actualization is then not to become *super* human but rather *fully* human, that is, finally and completely sane.

Conjoining Wilber with Maslow, we achieve self-actualization when we know our "Supreme Identity" as oneness with all reality, and several Perennialists have theorized what a model of the psyche related to this total breakthrough—this ontological expansion—might look like. The history of this movement and its insights is, of course, beyond the scope of this small handbook on the perennial philosophy but Stanislav Grof's views in *The Holotropic Mind* is one place to start (Frances Vaughan and Roger Walsh's *Paths Beyond Ego* is another), offering an overview of what the psychology of the future might look like.

Grof, based on many years of experience as a clinical psychiatrist, describes the nature of the psyche as it would be when considered from within a "quantum view of reality" rather than a view based on strict materialism. Specifically, he describes three levels of consciousness and how they shape our lives: first is the *personal level*, including the everyday state of mind, along with that strata of the unconscious mind shaped by our personal history; second, the *transpersonal level*, including Jung's *collective unconscious*; and third, the *interpersonal level*, in which, he argues, we experience self-actualization as "cosmic consciousness," an awareness of all that we are integrated with all that there is. And here we find a view of the psyche and its potential for self-actualization in agreement with Wilber's "Supreme Identity" and Huxley's "unitive knowledge." From a quantum perspective, we are not, according to Grof, a discrete being walking around in a world of discrete objects (as our senses suggest and as our culture's materialism teaches us) but rather a "holomovement" of energy inside a gigantic, quantum interference pattern.

There's a lot of abstract conjecture here, but I hope to give some idea of the top end of where psychology might eventually take us, given that the possibilities, as well as our own potentialities, are both enormous and promising. In Grof's own words: "Over three decades of systematic studies of the human consciousness have led me to conclusions that many traditional psychiatrists and psychologists might find implausible if not downright incredible. I now firmly believe that consciousness is more than an accidental by-product of the neurophysiological and biochemical processes taking place in the human brain. I see consciousness and the human psyche as expressions and reflections of a cosmic intelligence that permeates the entire universe and all of existence. We are not just highly evolved animals with biological computers embedded inside our skulls; we are also fields of consciousness without limits, transcending time, space, matter, and linear causality."

With this vision of what's possible for the psyche—and psychology—now outlined, and moving toward some kind of summary, the important point to make is that all psychologists whose work broadly agrees with perennialism are arguing that there is a *positive unconscious*. Where Freud, Adler, and others argued we are influenced by the negative unconscious, mostly made up of our repressed—and therefore frustrated—drives for sex and power, transpersonal psychologists posit that there are also levels such as Jung's collective unconscious and the deeper levels of our being that also motivate our behavior. Again, mental illness, including neurosis and psychosis, may be caused not only by repressed desires but also by our frustrated need to self-actualize.

One danger of this level of frustrated development is that we may, in desperation, try to transcend our present limits in ways that are not productive, for instance by using dangerous drugs like cocaine or heroin, or by immersing ourselves in risk-taking activities that make us feel 'more alive.' These actions take us outside of our everyday consciousness but they do not lead to self-realization; moreover, they can generate a frustrated state of mind that incites more dangerous risk-taking, pushing us into a vicious cycle of seeking higher thrills. We go beyond ourselves but not in ways that lead to expansion of consciousness.

Where Freud viewed neurosis as rooted in a person's maladjustment to society, transpersonalists see the problem as rooted in her or his maladjustment to ultimate reality. Maslow argued that finding such an adjustment leads to the fulfillment of our meta-drives, and this, as the top end of sanity, should be the goal of psychiatry, rather than what we find today, which is an emphasis on assimilation to society's dictates and a conformity to its views of sanity.

What would this "more fully sane state" look like for the individual experiencing it? Where now we might create identity for ourselves via our nationality, job description, sexual orientation and/or family relationships (father, brother, son, etc.), in the fully-realized state we might set those concerns of one level of our psyche inside the meta-levels of ourself as a personality experiencing "Supreme Identity" with the cosmos and its foundation in the Ground of Being. In other words, and here I'm making a joke, when you attend a cocktail party and someone asks you who you are, if you can, with a straight face, truthfully reply, "I'm a *holo-movement* and living expression of the infinite Ground of Being, nice to meet you," then you will have fulfilled all your psyche's meta-drives and achieved the apex of Maslow's vision of sanity.

Today there is a cadre of transpersonal psychologists and researchers in the field of consciousness studies who take seriously that the potentialities of human consciousness are far greater than we general have suspected. For instance, Dr. Edward Kelly, professor of perceptual studies and psychiatry at the University of Virginia School of Medicine, theorizes that when UMEs occur they trigger what he terms ROSTA experiences of "retrieval of subliminal or transpersonal assets" useful to our lives, and his work, and that of several others, can be found in his edited volume *Irreducible Mind: Toward a Psychology for the 21st Century* (2009), a book I strongly recommend.

14

NATURE

"What the power of the Slowing taught me is what the Source of All is constantly yearning for: that each of us will know without doubt that we are loved, and that we are intimately, irrevocably part of the endless creation of love, and that we will join, with full freedom and consciousness, the joyous creativity that is Nature."

Gerald G. May

"There is no separate, inside self and no separate outside object, other or world. Rather, there is one seamless, intimate totality, always changing when viewed from the perspective of objects, never changing when viewed from the perspective of the totality."

Rupert Spira

In Part II, we briefly answered the question, "Where are we?" And, as beings who live in two dimensions, physical and metaphysical, we've said that the metaphysical substrate is without physical qualities, a Ground of Being that is beyond time and space. But what about the seemingly physical aspect of the world? Or, put another way, if the Ground is the universe's soul, what is the nature of nature's body-mind? And what is our place in it?

As we begin, let me point out that there are Perennialists and Neoperennialists who focus their inquiry exclusively on the psychological and phenomenological characteristics of the UME, making no claims about the nature of existence. Consequently, here again we find the perennial philosophy as other than a monolithic viewpoint. But the majority of Perennialists have shared their ontological views of the world arounds us, and so I'll share some of the commonalities.

Is the natural world kindly disposed toward us or is it "out to get us?" Or, yet again, is it benignly indifferent? Could it possibly be that all of these things are true at the same time? Certainly, we all have moments when it seems more like one than the other, which is perhaps why in cultures that prefer to describe reality, including the natural world, with symbols, we find images and stories conveying this complex, paradoxical and often enigmatic possibility. For example, the Tantric goddess Kali of South Asia is commonly depicted with full breasts of milk, conveying her status as the nurturing "Mother" of all, but she also sports a necklace of severed human heads (along with a miniskirt of severed human arms!) to indicate her aspect of character as the Grim Reaper. Kali is the "Terrifying Mother" who brings all of her children into this world but then lets none of them escape, a potent symbol of the fact that life and death are intertwined aspects of one cosmic dance—what Ram Dass described as "the only dance there is." Such is the poetic power of symbols to weave opposites into a whole that confounds contradiction in ways that offend logic but satisfy our deeper sensibilities.

Even if we narrow the focus of our view to the street level of concern (or, more specifically, to the "jungle level" or "mountain level"), we see that nature is not wholly one or the other. Tennyson once wrote that nature is "Red of tooth and claw," indicating that whether or not nature is evil, it is at least often hungry, so blood will be spilled. However, nature is also, we can add, "Red of rose and strawberry." It takes away but it also gives back, and on balance it has been giving back to myriad creatures, including ourselves, for millions of years. In fact, if that wasn't true, life wouldn't exist at all.

Alan Watts once observed, "We don't 'come into' this world, we come out of it, as leaves from a tree." The surfaces of Jupiter and Pluto are most certainly inhospitable environments for human beings, but Watts believed this planet, Earth, is generally accommodating, for if it were not, we would not exist. Today we may have technologies to cope with hostile environments like those of the moon and Mars, but this is a very recent circumstance of our history. In the long run, we have existed because this planet has grown us just as your head is now growing hair. It's just what the world does.

We are a part of this world, not *apart* from it. Its gravity has defined the form of our skeleton; its air has decided the nature of our lungs; its sunlight has shaped our eyes; and its cycles of day and night have set the rhythms of our lives. We belong to this world in ways most of us overlook or take for granted, rarely realizing how deep and abiding is our connection.

I had this pointed out to me most clearly by a Kogi shaman from Columbia when we were both attending the Parliament of World Religions in Salt Lake City in 2015. The Kogi observed, "You Younger Brothers [this is what the Kogi call those who arrived in America after Columbus] think of your 'bodies' as your arms and legs. But I can cut off my arm and still live. I can even cut off my legs and live. But if I cut myself off from *this*," and here he reached for a glass of water on the table in front of him, "I will die." He then looked out at the audience and asked: "I cannot cut myself off from this and live. So where does my body really end?" We are intertwined with the world of water—and sunshine, and air, and plants—and his example makes this point crystal clear.

But what does all this have to do with the perennial philosophy? Just this: Perennialists generally agree that nature is on our side, even if we're not always on hers. Perhaps nature does not, in every instance, support our individual actions, especially if, as the Kogi believe, we perceive nature in a myopic way, doing as we wish; however, in the long run (and because our bodies are entwined with hers) her best interests are our own. Nature is the God-mirror reflecting back to us our true image, good or bad. Furthermore, because at the root of our being we are one with the root of nature's being, we, in the awakened state, are capable of realizing a God's Eye view of our circumstances. Whatever the seemingly local situation may be (within the limited purview of the body-mind), the expanded view is that the universe is configured as it should be.

This doesn't mean that we shouldn't act for social justice or earth justice on the scale of existence where our daily lives take place; indeed we should. It's simply to say that life and creation writ large, and from a God's eye view, are qualitatively *Good*. In fact, if we were to live our lives in balance with nature, as some cultures have done (and still do), this world could be paradise. Yes, we would still get sick and eventually die, and yes, we would know sorrow at the loss of those we love, but these events are part of the life-cycle. Furthermore, those changes and challenges can be more easily accepted if we also experience that aspect of ourselves that is Life itself, the root of all existence, including nature's.

One upshot of the view that life is—ultimately and on balance—*Good* is that time spent in nature is often championed by Perennialists as a means to awaken the unitive knowledge. In the nineteenth century, adherents of the Romantic movement believed this in spades, and many of them had views of nature similar to the Perennialists, including poets William Wordsworth, Ralph Waldo Emerson, Walt Whitman, and William Butler Yeats; naturalists Henry David Thoreau and W.H. Hudson; and landscape painters Caspar David Friedrich, Thomas Cole, and Fredrick Church. They (and here I'm naming only a few) immersed themselves in the beauty of nature to trigger experiences of the "Sublime," moments of spiritual insight or resonance with the Sacred Wild. Since nature, from their perspective, is not only Good but Beautiful, they considered its grandeur a trigger for awakening themselves to both. Their pathway to transcendence was to drop deeply into nature's forms, including its oceans, mountains, forests and sky. Today some people, including myself, label this the "yoga of awe." It is based in aesthetic experience and generates a close cousin of mystical experience.

Others too have embraced time spent in nature as their pathway, viewing its mountains and forests as their cathedrals. Lao Tzu, for example, explained in the *Tao Te Ching* that nature is permeated by a sacred force, the Tao, with which we must come into harmony by "reconciling ourselves to the inevitable." This force—which George Lucas later used as the model for "The Force" of the Jedis—preceded the world of things but now flows through them, bringing balance and harmony to this diverse world whenever imbalance occurs. Baptizing ourselves in the rhythms of nature solicits the call of the Tao within us, bringing our patterns of thought and action into tune with the cycles of the world. Even if we do not see or hear the Tao, it acts upon us and intuition opens us to its flow, since we too, at our roots, are part of nature. This is Lao Tzu's message and we find it described beautifully in the pages of Thoreau's *Walden* or today the writings of Terry Tempest Williams.

Some Perennialists see this nature mysticism as inferior to other yogas, including the pathways of meditation and devotion to God, but others trust it bears the same fruit and better accommodates those who find solace in the great outdoors. Do you like to hike, paddle, or surf? Do you find yourself delighting in nature's intimacy, intricacy and grandeur? Do you feel more present and more yourself when you're in the woods? Perhaps you're this type of yogi, this type of mystic, like Thoreau, John Muir, and Annie Dillard.

Some students tell me they are not spiritual, but then also tell me they love backpacking and camping. When I ask what they like about it, they often, and somewhat ironically, speak in very spiritual tones, remarking that they feel "more like themselves," that they feel a "deep connection to the earth," and that it pulls them "into the present." Consequently, I urge them to expand their definition of *spiritual* to include these sorts of experiences, letting nature nurture their wild hearts whenever possible.

Moving along, Perennialists generally characterize nature as *sentient*; that is, awake in one sense or another. For some Perennialists, this implies there is a God who is omniscient (aware of everything) and He, She, They, or It, as the author and controller of creation, is also omnipotent (all powerful). However, all Perennialists, including those who do not experience a personal God, believe this sentience is also a quality of the Ground of Being. Put another way, they believe the Ground of Being is consciousness itself, whether or not it is also conscious of things in the usual sense.

While considering nature's quality of *sentience*, some find an answer to Friedrich Schelling's intriguing question about creation, which is, "Why is there something rather than nothing?" Why does creation or manifestation exist at all? Why didn't the Divine Ground keep to itself, simply resting in its own limitless nature? Why arise into multiplicity, changing from nothing into something?

One common answer is that it was and is inclined, almost mechanically, to arise out of an inherent need to know itself. For some reason (that actually needs no reason at all), the Ground wishes to become aware of its own existence. In its unmanifest or quiescent state, it can *be* itself, and it can be consciousness *itself*, but without duality to establish a context, it cannot know such things in the usual sense of being "conscious of" something.

Let me explain. To use an analogy, sugar is sweet but doesn't know it's sweet because it doesn't have a tongue. It would need a tongue to taste its sweetness. Similarly, the Ground of Being (Paul Tillich called it, the "God behind God") may have generated this world of multiplicity to give itself a tongue. To be conscious of anything, a duality is required in which a *subject* can see, hear or otherwise become aware of an *object*. In the quiescent state of Nothingness or pure potentiality, the Ground had no such duality; consequently, it generated one (or perhaps the illusion of one) out of itself. Just as we may stand in front of a mirror to become aware of what we look like, creating an illusion of ourselves as an object of perception beyond ourselves, God, as Ibn Arabi and other Sufis maintain, created this universe to give a context for knowing his own nature. The natural world, then, is God's mirror, a way to know and express the Divine.

Some Perennialists see the creation story as a "one off," believing creation was a solitary event, starting with a "Big Bang" of some sort. Others believe creation has happened, as the Buddhists say, "since beginningless time," implying that there is a two-part cycle of quiescence and manifestation that occurs endlessly. The universe lifts up into existence and then, much later, it dissolves, over and over again. Furthermore, there is a sub-school across both that I've just mentioned that posits human beings as the clearest mirror in which the Sacred can glimpse itself. In this view, the Sacred becomes most aware of itself in the context of human form. Humans, if they are fully awake, are able to know that aspect of themselves that is synonymous with the Oversoul or Ground of Being, so when they wake up to what they truly *are*, the universe wakes up to what it truly *is*—sometimes in the same moment.

Digging into this point a bit deeper, there are Perennialists who believe we are now in a phase of the cosmic drama when the Ground or Oversoul, in its striving to know itself, is working to evolve a neurophysiology capable of that task. Over eons (after all, what's the rush if the Ground of Being is timeless?), it has been evolving increasingly sophisticated nervous systems that are increasingly capable of experiencing themselves as both body-minds and the Ground of Being. And so the motive force of spiritual evolution that drives a person to wake up is simultaneously the drive of the natural world to biologically evolve.

This school of the perennial philosophy (inside my definition of it), embracing what is called *evolutionary panentheism*, includes such theorists as Gerald Heard and Michael Murphy, and is in close agreement with earlier mystics such as Jacob Boehme, William Blake, Sri Aurobindo, and the German philosopher Friedrich Schelling. *Pantheists* (for example, Native Americans) believe the world is fecund with various spirits inhabiting trees, rivers, mountains, etc., while *panentheists* subscribe to the view that Spirit pre-exists and transcends all physical creation, though it's also imminent in creation. However, *evolutionary panentheists* argue that via physical evolution the universe is generating beings who can awaken "God" or Ultimate Reality to his, her or Its own nature.

Schelling, Aurobindo, Boehme, and others have argued that we are becoming God's fingertips, eyes, and ears. We are becoming the "tongue that can taste the sugar" of God's own nature. Alan Watts, who entertained this possibility, often spoke of the universe's eternal story as "God playing hide and seek with himself." The Ground of Being falls (in the biblical sense) into the world of multiplicity and ignorance, only to discover later, in the context of being human (and who knows what other creatures), that the whole drama was a cosmic game (called *lila* or the "divine play" in India)—a game that's revealed every time a human being wakes up to what's really going on.

Predicated on this view, Gerald Heard (in *Pain, Sex and Time,* 1939) and Michael Murphy (in *The Future of the Body,* 1992) envision the possibility of a future in which enlightened humans live in peace with the world; however, other Perennialists are not so optimistic. Huston Smith and Aldous Huxley, for example, subscribed to the view that, "The more things change, the more they stay the same." Moving from the Ground to the "ground beneath our feet," neither writer predicted a Golden Age looming on the horizon, pointing out that only a few people in every generation have ever woken up to their true natures. "It's like a beach ball," Huston Smith once explained to me. "There may be one half of the beachball facing the sky, but the other half is always under water." Just as there are only a few musical geniuses in each generation, Huston believed there might only be a few people with a talent for waking up.

Reflecting on who is right about this, the good news may be that most Perennialists see it as a non-issue. It can be intellectually entertaining to speculate about (are we the context for Nature's or God's own awakening? Are we on the verge of a mass upgrade in consciousness? Is enlightenment simply an ability humans can develop, though it has no significance other than that it gives us perspective on our own lives?), but do we need answers to these questions before we can wake up ourselves? All agree we don't.

Someday, to some extent, we may know what's possible, given that time will tell, but for now the realizable goal is the personal experience of the unitive knowledge. This awakening, by as many of us as possible, will provide nature and its creatures—including us—with the best chance of survival. Infused with the gift of insight, including an awareness of the interconnectivity of all life, I think humans will find themselves wanting harmony more than they now do control or dominance. In the meantime, it's wise to remember that nature will have the last word on all this, for as a popular bumper sticker points out (using a baseball analogy), "Nature Bats Last." We will either find ways to live in harmony with nature or we will continue to make a hard bed for us to sleep in.

15

ART

"Art enables us to find ourselves and lose ourselves at the same time."

Thomas Merton

"It's not what you look at that matters, it's what you *see*."

Henry David Thoreau

I taught philosophy and world religions at the Maine College of Art & Design for nearly thirty years, but one thing that always interested me was how often students, all of whom were deeply engaged in art-making, rarely stopped to ask themselves what art *is*. Based on the momentum of concepts endemic to our culture, they had an ambient sense of what it might be, but when—in my course on aesthetics—I would stand before them and ask point blank what they meant when they said "art," I would generally get blank stares or one or two comments of this sort, "Well, you know—it's ART!"

Reflecting on the subject, they quickly realized how vague and various were their unexplored understandings and, to their credit, rolled up their sleeves for new inquiries, often causing me to do the same—since after all, even professors have their illusions and limitations.

But now I ask you what is art? What is art *for*? What does art *do*? What does it actually mean to say something is beautiful? What is the nature of that experience we sometimes have with art and music that sends shivers up our spines? Why are we so drawn to these experiences?

Having taught at an art college, these questions have a deep significance for me. Everyday as I walked to my office, I passed by paintings and sculptures that stopped me in my tracks. Such creativity! Forever is never long enough to express what goes on in the human spirit. Conversely, sometimes these expressions come in such beautiful forms we feel there's nothing more that needs to be said. For example, for more than fifty years I have visited a particular painting in the Metropolitan Museum of Art, whenever I'm in New York City. I first saw Jules Bastien-Lepage's extraordinary "Joan of Arc" in 1970 during a college field trip. I didn't know why it caught me but it did, and still does. It is gigantic, life-size, showing Joan standing in her garden with an extraordinary look on her face. When I first saw it, it inspired the same expression on my face, a look of silent wonder, rapture, transcendence and transfiguration. I'm still mesmerized by that painting—as, no doubt, the artist intended. But what is this power of art, and what causes it?

Answering these questions is the province of that sub-discipline of philosophy labeled *aesthetics*. Aesthetics deals with those *qualia* issues related to art, and as we've discussed earlier, the scientific method gets no traction on these issues. Is a painting beautiful or otherwise aesthetically significant? Science has no way of telling. Consequently, and because there is no scientific way to measure art, prove its value or even explain what it *is*, theories of art range widely. Indeed, there is no consensus in our culture—or between cultures—about what makes a piece of art *significant*, suggesting for many post-modern philosophers that there can be no universal explanation of art's value. And I'll agree they may be right.

There is also no consensus between Perennialists on the nature of art. For example, the interesting visionary artist Alex Grey, himself an avowed Perennialist, argues in his book, *The Mission of Art* (1998), that Michelangelo was history's "most fully realized artist," while Frithjof Schuon, in *The Transcendent Unity of Religions* (1946), tell us he abhors all Renaissance painters, including Michelangelo. Both Grey and Schuon are Perennialists but their disagreement illustrates how far apart they can be on the subject of art. But when we look closely, we find points of agreement, especially when discussing the question, "What is art for?"

Aesthetic experience is likely the cousin of mystical experience. In fact, it is likely deeply akin to it, for what, after all, is the difference? Perhaps the distinction between the two relates more to how wide or deep our mental aperture has opened during a particular experience (of either variety) than it does with the general nature of the experiences themselves—especially given that the two varieties sometimes become one. People often report that profound beauty transported them into a noetic state similar to—if not synonymous with—the unitive mystical experience. For instance, Warner Allen relates in his *The Timeless Moment* (1946) an instance when mystical insight arose while listening to a symphony. The details are worth noting:

> Rapt in Beethoven's music, I closed my eyes and watched a silver glow which shaped itself into a circle with a central focus brighter than the rest. ... There was an impression of drawing strength from a limitless sea of power and a sense of deepening peace. The light grew brighter but was never dazzling or alarming. I came to a point where time and motion ceased. ... [I was] absorbed in the Light of the Universe, in Reality glowing like fire with the knowledge of itself, without ceasing to be one and myself, merged like a drop of quicksilver in the Whole yet still separate as a grain of sand in the desert. The peace that passes all understanding and the pulsating energy of creation are one in the centre in the midst of conditions where all opposites are reconciled.

Perennialists commonly agree that aesthetic experience can transport us into a transfigured state as surely as can a meditation practice. Conversely, they also believe unitive experiences often trigger moments of exquisite beauty. And this deep similarity between mystical and aesthetic experience is specifically what caused the poet Friedrich Schiller to think of art as the savior of humankind, for, like mystical experience, sublime moments not only reveal beauty but via beauty they lift us up to peak experiences of reality, inspiring our spiritual and moral growth. Based on Friedrich Schelling's "Transcendental Idealism" (itself arguably a form of perennialism), Schiller shared a theory of art's mission in *On the Aesthetic Education of Man* (1794). There, in no uncertain terms, he describes art as the best way forward, doing what science cannot. Later he would also express this view in his poetry, telling us that, "Only through beauty's gate can you penetrate the land of knowledge."

Expanded consciousness leads to upgrades in our *qualia*-related sensitivities, including moral improvements, an opening of the heart, an increase of meaning, and an improved awareness of one's place in the world. And so, art, because it can eventuate expanded consciousness, can be a type of yoga, a means of reaching enlightenment. Artists are, if you don't mind the play on words, always "drawing" themselves into a deeper perspective, while art appreciators use art to instigate their own aesthetic and noetic awakenings. Consequently, for those in-the-know, art, music and literature are not simply entertainment or decoration. Ultimately, they are not recreational but *re-cre-ational*, a way to see with new eyes and hear with new ears.

However, if Perennialists agree on the general purpose of art, what is the crux of their disagreement? Dissension tends to arise when we move from the goal of art toward a consideration of how art works; in other words, if Beauty (broadly conceived and with much nuance) can awaken us, as Schiller argued, what are the best images or forms for doing that? Are there colors, shapes, proportions, and arrangements that comprise a formal language of beauty? Is there imagery of some sort that can reliably awaken the sublime experience? Are there artworks from the past that prove this to be so, inescapably inspiring a sense of beauty whenever *anyone*—of any cultural background—sees them? Many Perennialists, including Alex Grey and Schuon, believe there *are*, and so they have worked out systems to convey their respective viewpoints or formalistic grammars of art. I, by the way, am not so sure, but we'll get to that.

For traditionalists like Schuon, there are time-tested tomes that describe such grammars, including Islamic texts advocating for complex geometrical patterns, while disallowing pictorial representations of Allah or the prophets. There are Tibetan manuals describing a dizzying array of Buddhas, each with its own iconography that must be conveyed perfectly (and, in contrast to Islamic sensibilities, mostly depicting human-like figures). This discrepancy in the grammars of the two cultures is not thought to be a problem by traditionalists because the grammar of art may change from culture to culture, as do the grammars of language, while each still enlivens the aesthetic experience for its constituency. In fact, a society's iconography and grammar have arisen in a specific context that makes them best suited to fulfilling the mission of art for that particular people.

Citizens of these societies know exactly how to interpret the forms and imagery of their artists' paintings, as they know how to interpret the forms of their spoken language, while the paintings and sculptures of another culture might leave them confused or offended. In the same way that there are two levels of religion, as we've discussed in the "Religion" chapter, there are, for the traditionalists, differences among cultures on the *exoteric* level of the outward forms of artworks, while on the *esoteric* level of aesthetic or mystical awakening we find the same experience. To make this clear, Chinese brush painting may seem simplistic and child-like to someone from Europe but it eventuates the same experience of "beautiful" for the Chinese as do the paintings of Rembrandt or Monet for Europeans. Summing up, we find agreement between cultures on the level of the sublime experience but disagreement about which forms best trigger it.

There are also Perennialists who endorse a formalist perspective, in ways similar to that of modernism, believing that there is a universal grammar of art underlying the outward forms of all cultures. Seeing the situation similar to Kandinsky and the Bauhaus movement, they argue that though the traditional texts describing the best forms disagree with each other, we can still recognize a universal grammar across the traditions—relying on such elements as color-relationships, composition, proportion, and the tension between symmetry and asymmetry. Like modernists from Gertrude Stein to Clement Greenberg, these Perennialists believe we are viscerally drawn to replicate certain forms and arrangements almost as we are biologically inclined to continuously seek out sugar, salt and fat. Sugar and salt taste good in all societies; likewise, there are colors, color relationships, and shapes we can't help but enjoy. It's as though these things are on the hard drives of our brains, rather than being acquired tendencies.

Perennialists who believe in a universal grammar of art also often contend that we are drawn to certain visual forms, especially those of icons, personalities and animals, because they relate to trans-cultural archetypes residing in Jung's collective unconscious. For instance, we may not understand the specific iconography of Buddhists, Hindus, or the Hopi, but we respond viscerally to imagery that suggests the demonic or nurturing aspects of nature. Likewise, we are attracted to certain narratives in literature, such as that of the quest or the beleaguered hero, rich with metaphors and symbols—leading Joseph Campbell to refer to these symbols and metaphors as "the language of the soul."

Without denying that there are forms likely to attract us, a third broad group of Perennialists argue that too much attention to the grammar of forms and colors (or notes, melodies and rhythms) may distract us from the true nature of art. Art is a means not an end, and no work of art can guarantee an aesthetic experience every time it's viewed. The viewer may or may not be transported into a sublime or noetic state depending on many conditions, including their sensitivity to such experiences. Consequently, and given that these latter theorists believe Beauty resides only in the experience itself, no masterpiece is thought to be actually or implicitly beautiful. No painting or sculpture can contain Beauty or deep aesthetic interest like a bucket can contain water. Beauty is not *inside* the painting; it's inside you and me. The painting only awakens an experience—if we're capable of having it. The painting is a means to an end, not an end in itself, and no work of art can trigger the beautiful experience in everyone.

This latter viewpoint, argued by Ananda Coomaraswamy in *The Dance of Shiva* (1918), and by Aldous Huxley in *The Doors of Perception* (1956), contends that all forms arise from the Ground of Being (as does everything else), and so all forms can lead us back into the experience of the Ground, with no particular form or compositional relationship foolproof. In this view, forms are specific to cultures (as is a culture's grammar or language) and each culture's forms act as springboards into the aesthetic or noetic experience for people of that culture. Symmetrical forms like Islamic "arabesques" may do the trick for Muslims, while asymmetrical forms, like those of Picasso, may work for others. Iconography rich in archetypes may provide a gateway to transcendence but so, after all, can a piece of colored glass discovered on the beach.

Regularly, we find ourselves collecting pieces of nonsense, such as feathers and interesting rocks, that may have no significance for others but remind us of a particular day, a close friend, or a significant experience. These are not great works of art and yet they still may have the power to invoke the sublime, i.e. a power to transport. Consequently, we again find an example of Stace's principle of "causal indifference" (first discussed in Chapter 7). Coomaraswamy, like Stace, argued that if something works, it works, and this is a viewpoint with which I agree. Whatever object awakens us to an experience of beauty or aesthetic engagement is a viable trigger and need not fit anyone else's criteria of art to be valuable. If an odd shaped rock on our bookshelf reminds (i.e. *re-minds*) us to the sublime, it "works."

So what is the bottom line for Perennialists on this subject? It is the irony that we regularly enjoy the mystical experience synonymous with aesthetic experience but then deny that mystical experience exists. We shed tears for the beauty of a sunset and we clap madly for a virtuoso performance, yet we claim that spiritual transfiguration isn't possible. Perennialists believe, as the Romantics once did, that art is more than entertainment. Perhaps we too should take art more seriously, even admitting its metaphysical potency? If we did so, one thing is certain: art and music programs in public schools would be better funded.

Materialists will argue that Perennialists are making this assumption based on the theory that we have an aspect of our being or consciousness that transcends our individual existence, but it's important to note that people are already making qualia decisions based on an unproven theory about what we are. There is no reason today why must accept the materialists' unproven platform for making qualia decisions as some sort of baseline to hold in place until Perennialists—or someone else—proves scientifically that consciousness exceeds the brain, especially when they have not proven that it doesn't. Furthermore, the noetic apprehension of our oneness with reality can be tested via your own instrument of inquiry, that is, by expanding your own minds experientially.

16

THE PERENNIAL PHILOSOPHY TODAY

"When you wake up to the Divine Consciousness within you and to your divine identity, you wake up simultaneously to the Divine Consciousness appearing as all other beings. And this is not poetry and this is not a feeling, this is a direct experience of the divine light living in and as all other beings."

Andrew Harvey

"[There is] nothing irrational about seeking the states of mind that lie at the core of many religions. Compassion, awe, devotion, and feelings of oneness are surely the most valuable experiences a person can have."

Sam Harris

$\mathcal{B}$*ack in chapter* 3, we took a look at Huxley's "Minimum Working Hypothesis" of the perennial philosophy, which became the platform theory for most early Perennialists and transpersonal psychologists. *In Paths Beyond Ego, the Transpersonal Vision* (1993), Roger Walsh and Frances Vaughan summarized this shared, four-point perspective, holding that "the world and all its creatures are expressions of an underlying divine reality; by appropriate training humans can come to know this reality; and they can recognize their unity with this divine ground. Finally, this recognition of the divine ground as our true nature is the highest goal of human existence." But does that platform still hold together for the perennial philosophy today? Do these four points continue to define or inform what is most characteristic of perennialism? I think they generally do, but that doesn't mean they can't be improved upon for clarity's sake.

We've noted disagreements over the details of these four points as we've moved along; for instance, some Perennialists believe that spiritual awakening is episodic (it comes and goes), while others argue it can be continuous and permanent; some say that point four, regarding our "highest goal," is an aspiration of the universe itself (in its hope to use the human mind to experience its own nature), while others believe awakening is simply a capacity of the mind beneficial to our health—and so on and so forth. Furthermore, we've seen that the repercussions of the four-point platform for topics like religion, psychology, and views of God (including atheism) have varied greatly, which, again, is why I've said perennial philosophy is not a siloed viewpoint. In fact, today, fifty years after the first big wave of interest, perennial philosophy is even more diverse and nuanced than ever before.

Today there are self-proclaimed "neo-perennialists" (Ken Wilber), "psychological perennialists" (Robert K.C. Forman), "soft perennialists" (Steve Taylor), advocates of "perennial wisdom" (Rabbi Rami Shapiro), exponents of "primordial philosophy" (Samuel Bendeck Sotillos), and other such sub-categories of Perennialism, and they have resulted, collectively, in a wider range of characteristic features. By cross-referencing those features, we can determine the commonalities of "family resemblance" in this now even larger family of theories.

Venturing my own minimum working hypothesis of the perennial philosophy as it stands today, I suggest this:

> The perennial philosophy is a family of theories surrounding the unitive mystical experience (UME), including its cross-cultural, continuously recurring and beneficial nature.

And to the family's most salient characteristics, I would add that Perennialists generally, but not always, believe:

(1) Consciousness, rather than materiality or physicality, is primary to the universe.

(2) Our personal experience of consciousness is not generated by the brain, but filtered by and received by the brain (more on this in a moment!)

(3) Consciousness is a variable and can be expanded in ways that are deeply beneficial.

(4) The unitive mystical experience or UME is the most broadly beneficial type of mystical experience.

(5) The religions of the world make very different claims, and the UME is *not* the core of all religion.

(6) Noetic experience is a valid way of knowing.

(7) The UME matters more than any theory about it.

(8) Aesthetic experience is closely related to mystical experience, including the UME, and may differ from it only in terms of intensity rather than kind.

(9) Theories of the UME should not contradict scientific facts.

(10) Improved traits of behavior matter more than flashy states of consciousness.

Other characteristics could be added, but my point is to list some key commonalities, beyond any broad definition or hypothesis, to draw out a general description of the perennial philosophy today.

Do all self-described Perennialists believe all of the characteristics listed above? No, nor is it necessary that they do. A Perennialist may only believe in a smattering of them, in the same way that a member of an actual family may only have some of the facial and bodily features common to their family. She may have dad's nose and mom's hair color but otherwise differ from her siblings in terms of the family's most characteristic features. Similarly, we find Perennialists who believe there are higher states of consciousness, that human beings self-actualize by reaching them, and that "traits matter more than states," but who—as is the case for psychological Perennialists—make no claims about the existence of God, the Sacred, or a Ground of Being outside the human head. They acknowledge that the UME occurs cross-culturally and is likely to have psychological benefits, but take no stand on the nature of existence (which is why I've made no ontological claims in my own minimum working hypothesis above).

I begin this chapter on contemporary Perennialists with the above explanation because it's important to keep in mind that today's Perennialists do not all believe in exactly the same theory (nor do I believe they ever did). They belong to the family but not all family members look exactly alike.

Using the characteristics I've listed, I personally identify a great number of perennial philosophers in our world today. These fall into a variety of groups, including everyday folks whose personal worldview is akin to Perennialism even when they don't realize it (for instance, the majority of yoga and meditation teachers). But among theorists in the realm of religious studies, philosophy, psychology, science, and spirituality, I generally place Perennialists in two groups: those who self-identify as Perennialists, and those whose views are simply a very close fit.

The sheer numbers that exist in both columns is too great for me to list and describe all of them, but in the former column, for instance, we find Richard Rohr, Rabbi Rami Shapiro, Mirabai Starr, Kurt Johnson, Joan Borysenko, Deepak Chopra, William Richards, Ralph Hood, Karen Armstrong, Stuart Sovatsky, Chris Grosso, Miri Albahari, Ken Wilber, Andrew Harvey, Alex Grey, and Charlie Tart, while in the latter column I would place Marianne Williamson, Sam Harris, Lynne McTaggert, Rupert Spira, Dean Radin, Daniel Goleman, James Fadiman, Rupert Sheldrake, Philip Goff, Peter Russell, Jeffrey Kripal, Bernardo Kastrup, Marjorie Woollacott, Edward Kelly, and almost every transpersonal psychologist working today. Sorry to all these folks in advance if I've put them in the wrong column or if they wish to argue that they don't fit into either. I'm just trying to give the reader an idea of how generally prevalent Perennialism is—at least if identified by significant agreement with the list of characteristics above (and with weight placed on the UME and its beneficial effects).

Though a careful critique of the various theories of those mentioned above exceeds the project of this book, let's look briefly at a few to get a sense of how the perennial philosophy now takes form. Specifically, we'll look into the following trends or areas of focus, inviting the reader to follow up on their own—if they wish—by researching the specific theorists mentioned: (1) Consciousness is fundamental to reality (whether as a Ground of Being, a pervasive quality of the natural world, or both); (2) our everyday experience of consciousness is not generated by the brain but filtered by, received by, or contextualized by the brain; (3) experiencing the UME is greatly beneficial to our mental and physical health; (4) awakened consciousness catalyzes social activism, and social activism catalyzes awakened consciousness; (5) Religion and spirituality can be re-enlivened via direct experience of the UME; and (6) Perennialist theories form one basis for interpreting UMEs occurring during psychedelic experience. Let's take these one at a time, keeping in mind that I'm giving only brief overviews.

(1) Consciousness is fundamental to reality.

The trend here is that consciousness is a primary element of existence and exceeds the limits of the human brain. Within this trend the two general viewpoints are that consciousness is either a Ground of Being/undifferentiated consciousness giving rise to everything else (in philosophy, a form of transcendental idealism) or consciousness constitutes the intrinsic nature of the physical universe—but has no transcendental aspect—and so is found in everything, everywhere (panpsychism). Of these two views, both of which oppose the materialist position that everything is made out of matter, transcendental idealism is closest to Huxley's and that of the other early Perennialists. Huxley's "Mind at Large" fills the universe with consciousness but it also transcends the universe, and that specific position (inclusive of a Ground of Being) is defended today by a range of theorists, including scientists like Nick Herbert (quantum physics), Rupert Sheldrake (biology), and Shantena Sabbadini (quantum physics); philosophers including Miri Albahari, Bernardo Kastrup, and Peter Russell; and scholars of religious studies such as Jeffery Kripal, Paul Marshall, G. William Barnard, Jorge Ferrer, and, frankly, me.

(2) Our everyday experience of consciousness is not generated by the brain but filtered by, received by or contextualized by the brain.

This trend is often presented as closely related to the first trend, as we're about to see, and of those scholars just mentioned, most would definitely fall into this category also. Furthermore, I would add to the list Marjorie Woollacott (neurophysiology), Edward Kelly (neurobehavioral sciences), and Eben Alexander (neurosurgeon).

In chapter 3 we discussed the Ground of Being and the view that Being itself is fundamentally a field of undifferentiated, absolute Consciousness. In summary, philosophically speaking, the majority of Perennialists hold the view that consciousness is fundamental to reality and exceeds the brain. Consciousness or "Mind at Large" is what enlivens our minds and is expressed through our minds, and this position stands in contrast to the materialists' "production" model that our brains create consciousness directly and are the sole locales of consciousness in an otherwise wholly unconscious universe. In their model, consciousness is an epiphenomenon or secondary effect of the brain as smoke is a by-product of fire or a foamy head is an epiphenomenon of a glass of beer. But quantum physicists including Herbert and Sabbadini, neuroscientists including Kelly, Woollacott, and David E. Presti—and scholars of comparative mysticism including Marshall, Barnard, and Kripal—have argued back that a "transmission" or "filter" theory seems more likely. And it's interesting to note here that both Kelly and Woollacott contend such theories make at least as much sense of the neuroscientific data. So let me explain their shared viewpoint.

Back in 1954, in *The Doors of Perception*, Huxley wrote that he agreed with "the eminent Cambridge philosopher" C.D. Broad in believing that Henri Bergson, the French philosopher, had been correct to say, in Broad's words, that the "function of the brain and nervous system is primarily *eliminative* and not productive. Each person is at each moment capable of remembering all that has ever happened to him and of perceiving everything that is happening everywhere in the universe. The function of the brain and nervous system is to protect us from being overwhelmed and confused by this mass of largely useless and irrelevant knowledge." Huxley then placed Bergson's theory into the context of his Perennialist view, writing: "According to such a theory, each one of us is potentially Mind at Large [undifferentiated and all-pervasive Consciousness]. But in so far as we are animals, our business is at all costs to survive. To make biological survival possible, Mind at Large has to be funneled through the reducing valve of the brain and nervous system. What comes out at the other end is a measly trickle." In brief, the position is that our senses didn't evolve in ways to make us aware of *everything*; they developed to show us *enough*, helping us to find food—and avoid becoming food. For the sake of survival, we've needed to reduce consciousness into a narrowly focused increment.

Related to the filter theory of consciousness is the "transmission" theory, which also holds that our brains do not directly produce our awareness. The basic idea is that the brain is a machine that makes possible an isolated experience of consciousness, but consciousness itself exists outside our heads. It is coming from elsewhere. So the brain functions, as Bergson once argued, like a radio, in that radios do not generate the programming they make possible, they receive the programs transmitted from outside themselves. This is why Jeffery Kripal, a leading scholar of religious studies today, has referred to the brain as a "superevolved neurological radio" in his book, *The Flip* (2019)—a book which deals mainly with how filter and transmission theories of the brain are "flipping" our cultural worldview away from the materialist position. For an excellent overview of transmission theories in general, and the science behind them, see Edward Kelly, Adam Crabtree, and Paul Marshall's edited volume, *Beyond Physicalism* (2015).

The point I wish to leave you with regarding this particular area of concern is that it has great explanatory power when considering why the UME is said to trigger a burning desire to help others. If we exist in an existential state of inter-being and shared consciousness with all creatures and all things, they are "us" and we are "them." The UME helps us to escape the view of ourselves as isolated beings—and opens us to our integral relationship with the world.

(3) Experiencing the UME is greatly beneficial to our mental and physical health.

In the chapter on psychology, we dealt with this point in some detail, so we need not belabor it here. The job is really to identify those today who emphasize this area of concern. There are currently a great number of transpersonal psychologists and wellness experts touting the benefits of the UME, and who interpret that experience in ways that agree with perennialism. Specifically, Mirabai Starr (a direct disciple of Ram Dass) focuses on how spiritual awakening helps relieve the effects of trauma, and how trauma can actually trigger spiritual awakening; Marianne Williamson works with how women can transcend the pernicious effects of patriarchy by accessing higher levels of consciousness and deeper levels of self; Rabbi Rami Shapiro and Chris Grosso write about how consciousness expansion and the "perennial wisdom" can lead to addiction recovery; Joan Borysenko, an expert in psychoneuroimmunology (dealing with the effects of our thoughts on our immune system), describes how self-actualization leads to better mental health and, in turn, better health in general; and Don Hanlon Johnson, Stephen Cope, Elizabeth Gibson, and others in the field of *somatics* or "bodywork" use dance, yoga, breath work, movement, and massage to access our oneness with reality as a means of improving general wellness.

(4) *Awakened consciousness catalyzes social activism, and social activism catalyzes awakening.*

Mirabai Starr, whom I've just mentioned, once wrote that when you "turn your gaze toward the holy mystery you once called God, the mystery follows you back out into the world." Today we're seeing a range of Perennialists whose work transcends issues of personal wellness to address issues of social justice, world peace, poverty, and hunger. For instance, Rami Shapiro, who works with people in recovery, has said, "Knowing God isn't knowing through theological speculations about God but rather knowing God directly, the way a ray of sunlight knows the sun," and as rays of the divine light, Shapiro challenges people to channel that light back into the world. "You are the way God feeds the hungry," he explains, and the way God "clothes the naked, frees the native, and heals the sick."

Following a nearly identical logic, Richard Rohr is an American Franciscan priest who founded the Center for Action and Contemplation in Albuquerque, New Mexico. His website tells us, "His work's essential message focuses on the union of divine reality with all things and the human potential and longing for this union." Moreover, he argues in agreement with the majority of Perennialists that what we need most today is not new ideas but the expanded consciousness that gives birth to them. "We do not think ourselves into new ways of living," he explains, "we live ourselves into new ways of thinking."

One last person to name here is hardly the least of the trend: Andrew Harvey is a well-known mystic of the Perennialist variety whose efforts focus on social justice and global concern. Rather than simply following our hearts, Harvey recommends we also "follow our heartbreak," giving time and attention to whatever dire circumstance most disturbs us. He is an author and spiritual teacher of international reknown. "Sacred Activism," he tells us, "is the fusion of the mystic's passion for God with the activist's passion for justice, creating a third fire, which is the burning sacred heart that longs to help, preserve, and nurture every living thing."

(5) Religion and spirituality can be re-enlivened via direct experience of the UME.

In several places, including the chapter on "Religion," I've mentioned the traditionalist school of Perennialism, including their view that the unitive experience of our oneness with reality is at the core of the great mystical traditions. For them, understanding what Frithjof Schuon called "the transcendent unity of religion" offers a commonality between the faiths—though they also contend that on the level of scriptures, beliefs, rituals, music and culture, the religions are distinctly different—and differences are to be respected. Each tradition offers spiritual sustenance and shared values to its specific community, and these traditions should not be compromised into a watered-down universalism. However, the UME illuminates the structures of religion with deep noetic experience, insuring they not devolve into sets of arid and robotic customs. Theorists of the traditionalist school today, including Reza Shah-Kazemi, Harry Oldmeadow, Seyyed Housein Nasr, Samuel Bendeck Sotillos, and Jennifer Casey, participate in their native religions, but congregate from time to time to discuss what they consider the heart of the mystical traditions.

Though most Perennialists are either non-religious or seeking spiritual community outside of organized religion, there are a number of theorists, unaffiliated with the traditionalist school, who also argue the value of the perennial philosophy for religious life. Karen Armstrong, for instance, describes how mystical awakening reinvigorated her Catholic faith. She was once a conservative Catholic nun but later moved into a liberal faith that embraced mystical awakening and the wisdom of other traditions. She diverges from the traditionalists in that she credits mystical insight with breaking her out of her dogmatic slumber, re-enlivening her Catholicism not by affirming its established structures but by calling them into question. This tendency, to view Perennialism as a force for liberalizing religion, is shared by Rami Shapiro and Richard Rohr (Jew and Catholic, respectively), whom we've already met. Shapiro refers to himself as a "holy rascal" and encourages "holy rascality," urging his congregants and readers to challenge outdated structures of mind and institution. He's against the "fear-based, demonizing, alienating, and intrinsically violent" worldviews of "Big Religion," hoping to replace "ignorance with wisdom and fear with love." Rohr's views on the need to liberalize religion—and the value of Perennialism for accomplishing that—are very similar. Both, in resonance with Karen Armstrong, live inside their religion but exceed its boundaries.

(6) Using Perennialist theories to help interpret UMEs occurring during psychedelic sessions.

Here we stumble into another large focus of interest today—deserving of its own book—but for now, let me simply put a few stakes in the ground as an introduction to the topic. We can begin by noting that Huxley and the other early Perennialists all believed that psychedelic substances can sometimes trigger UMEs indistinguishable from those that occur naturally—and that these UME's have definite value for psychological therapy and personal growth. Huxley, Grof, Watts, Ram Dass (as Richard Alpert), Huston Smith, and Frances Vaughan wrote no less than ten books on the subject, all based on their direct, positive experiences with psychedelics. Vaughan later wrote of her journey with psilocybin:

I had an academic background in philosophy and comparative religion, but I realized that mystical teachings had now taken on an added dimension. My perception seemed to have shifted from a flat, two-dimensional intellectual understanding of the literature, to a three-dimensional sense of immersion in the mystical reality.

The perennial philosophy and the esoteric teachings of all time suddenly made sense. I understood why spiritual seekers were instructed to look within, and the unconscious was revealed to be not just a useful concept, but an infinite reservoir of creative potential. I felt I had been afforded a glimpse into the nature of reality and the human potential within that reality, together with a direct experience of being myself, free of illusory identification and constriction of consciousness.

Huston Smith, writing in the *Journal of Philosophy* in 1964, offered what would become their shared conclusion ever after: "When the fact that drugs can trigger religious experiences becomes incontrovertible, discussion will move to the more difficult question of how this fact is to be interpreted."

Sadly, research supporting the view that drugs could trigger religious experiences soon came to a grinding halt when the U.S. Government made the use of psychedelics illegal, even for scientific research. Between 1970 and 2000, this prohibition held in place, but when it slowly lifted, several scientific studies picked up where the earlier studies left off. Among these, the most important for the topic at hand was the 2005 study by Roland Griffiths and William Richards at Johns Hopkins Medical School. Specifically, Griffiths, Richards, and their team found that a single dose of psilocybin triggered long-lasting mystical experiences in thirty-six middle-aged volunteers, all of whom had never tried a psychedelic before. Two-thirds of that group placed their trip as one of the most profound spiritual events of their life, while one third claimed it as their number one moment of awakening—sometimes experiencing, according to Griffiths, "pure awareness, infinite love, tenderness and peace."

Over the years that followed that first study, Richards teamed up with Griffiths and others on further studies, often acting as a sitter for test subjects as they underwent their psychedelic sessions. Then, in 2016, he published his conclusions about the spiritual import of psychedelics in his book, *Sacred Knowledge: Psychedelics and Religious Experience.* "The evidence presented in this book represents a strong swing of the theoretical pendulum back toward the so-called perennialist perspective," Richards argued, and "there is good reason to affirm that there is indeed an eternal dimension of awareness deep in the core of the human mind where creativity, love, and beauty reign supreme."

Richards and Griffiths became the primary instigators of what is commonly termed the "Psychedelic Renaissance" (joined by Charles Grob, Anthony Bossis, and others), and today there is a cadre of figures, including the artists Alex and Alison Grey, and musicians Brian Eno and East Forest, who promote the Perennialist interpretation of UMEs occurring with psychedelics. It is important to keep in mind that psychedelic experience is a subset of life experience in general, and no life experience affords only one possible interpretation. Furthermore, not all psychedelic experiences are of the UME—or even positive or enjoyable—so there's no reason to assume that taking a pill will *necessarily* lead to spiritual awakening. Having said that, there is also no reason to believe that it sometimes cannot. My view, based on substantial personal experience, is that it *can.*

Let me end this short summation of the trend by saying that though the perennial philosophy is not the only way to interpret psychedelic experience, it is *one* way, and, I would argue, a compelling one. In support of the position that the UME experienced under psychedelics has value, I add David Yaden and Andrew Newberg's statement in *The Varieties of Spiritual Experience* (2022) that, "Some psychedelic studies [e.g. Barrett et al., 2015] have found that it is the first 'mystical' factor [discerned from questionnaires filled out after the subjects' sessions], which includes items related specifically to feelings of unity, that is most predictive of later positive outcomes like well-being." This finding, coming along nearly seventy years after *The Doors of Perception,* wouldn't have surprised Aldous Huxley at all.

EPILOGUE

"The spiritual journey is individual, highly personal. It can't be organized or regulated. It isn't true that everyone should follow one path. Listen to your own truth."

Ram Dass

"We are living through the most exciting, challenging and most critical time in human history. Never before has so much been possible; and never before has so much been at stake."

Peter Russell

What more needs to be said? Mostly I want to remind the reader that truth for all perennial philosophers, as for all mystics, is experiential, and no book of ideas—including this book—can be its equivalent. Some Perennialists believe the universe is too complex for our minds to comprehend and explain, while others believe it *can* be described, at least potentially, but all insist that no explanation can replace the value of noetic awakening. The direct experience of the "unitive knowledge" is its own legitimate way of knowing. Books can present conceptual approximates of this truth, and they can provide reasons for why the experience is valuable, but they are, in the final analysis, nothing more than that. They are approximates. Books and lectures point the way to awakening but they should not be sanctified or enshrined as unimpeachable dogmas.

My favorite story related to this is a Zen parable about two monks who are hiking up a mountain trail. The going is tough and they are struggling to catch their breath, so the younger of the two monks, who has been lagging behind, pauses to sit on a log and catch his breath. As he recovers, he straightens his back and looks ahead to find his master. Fortunately, the older monk has stopped not far ahead. He too is catching his breath. His student sees that the old man is smiling and pointing at something over the top of a pine tree. Following the direction of the old monk's finger, the young monk sees a bright pink moon rising into the sky, and the sight is so splendid he gasps in amazement. Soon he joins his master and the two monks sit for a spell to enjoy the rosy moonlight.

The moral of this story, according to Zen tradition, is that books and teachings are like fingers pointing to the moon of noetic awakening. They can direct us toward the truth but they are not the truth—at least, not of the noetic sort. Consequently, if we raise descriptions of the Sacred to the status of the Sacred itself, we get stuck on the conceptual level, mistaking the finger for the moon. A danger of words is that we can become entangled in them, asking our experiences to conform to their grammatical structures and conceptual frameworks, which in many cases are structures formed in ignorance of awakening. Note that in the Gnostic scriptures of Christianity, Jesus advised his disciples to avoid all dogmatic interpretations, even of his own teachings, "lest you be bound by them." In that same spirit, it would be better to burn this book than make a Bible of it. Best to let it serve as a finger pointing to the moon—a moon that will rise only when your mind is open at full aperture.

Meanwhile, don't take my word for the view that consciousness can be expanded. You too have a mind capable of noetic experience, so launch your own experiments. Practice what Huxley and Huston Smith termed "mystical empiricism," allowing your own experiences to help confirm or deny whether or not there is a 'moon' in the sky and a world of light outside Plato's Cave. Become an expert, as Thoreau advised, in "home cosmography," finding your own way forward—even when using the thoughts of others to get a sense of where you'd like to go. Attend concerts, visit galleries, learn to meditate, practice yoga, spend time in the forest, climb mountains, learn to surf, fall deeply in love. Do whatever it is that wakes you up to deeper levels of what you are. Remember what Thaddeus Golas once wrote in *The Lazy Man's Guide to Enlightenment* (1972), that, "Enlightenment doesn't care how you got there." As another piece of advice, I strongly recommend that you use

William James' three-fold test for discerning the validity and value of your spiritual revelations. Do they have "immediate luminosity," "philosophical reasonableness," and "moral helpfulness?" If so, embrace them; if not, let them go and try something else. Furthermore, I recommend making spiritual friends as you travel. It's nice to have company along the way, for after all, as Ram Dass once said, "We're all just walking each other home."

Today we live in a time of great trepidation over myriad dangers including climate change, over-population and loss of habitat, but we also live in a time of tremendous opportunity. Never before in human history have so many people had so much freedom to explore such a broad range of philosophies, religions, psychologies and states of consciousness. Regarding the latter and based on adventures into meditative and psychedelic states of consciousness, we now have a significant population of people who understand directly that consciousness can be experienced in a range of states; that the most common state of consciousness has limitations and distortions; that consciousness can be expanded; and that developing our latent potentialities of consciousness may be our best chance of healing our dysfunctional—and often violent—relationships with each other and the planet.

Frances Vaughan and Roger Walsh once observed: "[W]e have created a global situation that demands unprecedented psychological and social maturation. In the past we could consume without depletion, discard without pollution, multiply without overpopulation, and fight without fear of extinction. In other words, we could act out our immaturities whereas now we need to outgrown them." The good news is, I firmly believe, we *can* outgrow them. Cultural and religious traditions can be respected (though a close friend of mine often remarks that, "Tradition is little more than peer-pressure from dead people!") but those traditions need no longer limit our explorations. Peter Russell wrote thirty years ago that, the "wisdom of the human psyche already exists in many spiritual traditions, philosophies and psychologies," but he added to this that such traditions "need to be pulled together and researched. This is not to advocate a return to the religions of the past, but to rediscover the sacred within us in the language and technologies of the twentieth century."

I believe he was right, and now we can add to his technologies those of the twenty-first century. Russell called our collective endeavor to wake up an "inner Manhattan Project." Let me thank you in advance for helping move that project forward! You are a person possessed of the amazing ability to know yourself—directly and experientially—as belonging to the universe on every level of your being. Accept the gift and celebrate it.

FURTHER READINGS

College professors often make the mistake of recommending too many books, so I'll only list a few, and only those I currently find most useful for a small library of the perennial philosophy.

Books on the perennial philosophy, in the order I recommend them:

> Huston Smith, *Forgotten Truth*
> Ken Wilber, *The Spectrum of Consciousness*
> Alan Watts, *The Book*
> Lex Hixon, *Coming Home*
> Aldous Huxley, *The Divine Within*

Six other books useful for understanding the perennial philosophy and its implications:

> Ram Dass, *Be Here Now*
> Stanislav Grof, *The Cosmic Game*
> Jacob Needleman, *The Sword of Gnosis*
> Dana Sawyer, *Huston Smith: Wisdomkeeper*
> Wayne Teasdale, *The Mystic Heart*
> Frances Vaughan and Roger Walsh, eds. *Paths Beyond Ego: The Transpersonal Vision*

Recent works worth noting:

> Chris Grosso, *The Indie Spiritualist*

Kurt Johnson, *The Coming Inter-Spiritual Age*

William Richards, *Sacred Knowledge: Psychedelics and Religious Experiences*

Mirabai Starr, *God of Love* (discussing the Abrahamic religions)

Andrew Harvey, *The Direct Path* (a DIY guide to spiritual growth)

Rami Shapiro, *The Tao of Solomon: Unlocking the Perennial Wisdom of Ecclesiastes*

Rupert Sheldrake, *Ways to Go Beyond and Why They Work*

Richard Rohr, *What the Mystics Know*

Joan Borysenko, *Samadhi: The Unity of Consciousness and Existence*

Adyashanti, *The Impact of Awakening*

Rupert Spira, *The Nature of Consciousness*

ACKNOWLEDGMENTS

First, I'd like to express my gratitude to the many friends who commented on drafts of the original manuscript, steering me toward a clearer, richer and more expressive presentation of the ideas shared here. My thanks go out especially to Damon Ely, Terry Mason, Peter Stark, Claudia Turnbull, Carey Turnbull, Jim Alexander, Elizabeth Alexander, Emma Sawyer, Philip Goldberg, Rick Archer, Charlie Donahue, Paul Marshall, Jeff Kripal, Betty Stookey, Shantena Sabbadini, Uwe Rasch, Julian Piras, Mark Seelig, Maria Montenegro, Robert Diamante, and Suzanne Strempek Shea. I also wish to include a special thanks to Jon Sweeney, religion editor at Monkfish, who helped improve the flow of the chapters with several key suggestions. I'd also like to express my deep and heartfelt gratitude to a certain group of spiritual gangsters who inspired me to write this book, a group that includes my wife, Stephani, who believed from the beginning that I should write a book to clarify what the perennial philosophy is and isn't. Wonderful wife, you're the best.

Dana Sawyer is professor emeritus of philosophy and world religions at Maine College of Art & Design in Portland. He frequently teaches at the Esalen Institute in Big Sur, California and is author of many articles for *Tricycle*, *Parabola*, and *Yoga Journal*. In 2002, he published *Aldous Huxley: A Biography* (Crossroad Publishing). Subsequently, Sawyer was approached by Huston Smith to write his authorized biography, which came out as *Huston Smith: Wisdomkeeper* (Fons Vitae Press, 2014) and was endorsed, on its back cover, by Jeffrey Kripal, Deepak Chopra, and H.H. the Dalai Lama.

Printed in the USA
CPSIA information can be obtained
at www.ICGtesting.com
JSHW021937240524
63681JS00001B/4

9 781958 972298